"This book is full of ways ~~tial.~~ *Rethink Your Marketing* uses real world examples ~~and~~ tific research to back up its highly actionable strategies. If your business is stuck in low gear, this book will get you moving!"

– Roger Dooley, author of *Brainfluence*

"*Rethink Your Marketing* will help you break through plateaus and guide you to discover new opportunities for your business."

– Darren Hardy, Success Mentor to CEOs & Founding Publisher *SUCCESS Magazine*

"Tom has created a wonderfully concise, fun to read roadmap for all brands – no matter where they are in their life cycle – who are eager to 10X their growth. *Rethink Your Marketing* should be required reading for anyone working in a marketing role."

– Andrew Wilson, Account Executive, Google

"Tom tackles marketing challenges strategically, and always with the target audience in mind. His book helps you to take a step back and uncover new opportunities for your organization, creatively forging new and effective ways to connect with your audience and achieve your marketing goals."

– Howard Brodsky, Co-Founder, Chairman, and Co-CEO, CCA Global Partners

RETHINK YOUR MARKETING

7 STRATEGIES TO UNLEASH REVENUE GROWTH

TOM SHAPIRO

STRATABEAT, INC.

Published by Stratabeat, Inc.

https://stratabeat.com/

Cover design by Analilia Morales

ISBN 978-0-9991847-0-7 (paperback)

ISBN 978-0-9991847-1-4 (ebook)

Additional Resources:

https://rethinkyourmarketing.com/

CONTENTS

INTRODUCTION   vii

1. RETHINK YOUR AUDIENCE   1
2. RETHINK HOW THEY THINK   31
3. RETHINK YOUR GOALS   67
4. RETHINK YOUR MARKETING MIX   95
5. RETHINK YOUR METRICS   131
6. RETHINK YOUR REVENUE MODEL   161
7. RETHINK YOUR FUTURE   191

    CONCLUSION   225
    NOTES   227
    ABOUT THE AUTHOR   249
    ADDITIONAL RESOURCES   251

INTRODUCTION

The high jump is a signature track and field event with its origins rooted in the ancient Greek Olympics. (That is the eighth century B.C. for goodness' sake!) Over the next 2,000 years, innumerable athletes have taken countless high jumps.

The first *recorded* high jump took place in Scotland in the 19th century, with athletes clearing a bar height of approximately 5 feet 6 inches. Through the years, athletes have used the same general techniques to leap over the bar: either approaching the bar straight on or throwing both legs over the bar in a scissors technique and landing face down. Along the way, a straddle variation of the scissors technique was adopted, but it largely followed the principles of the original style.

As athletes grew bigger and stronger and perfected the standard techniques, the height they were able to reach rose as well. The increase was incremental, with the Olympic record rising by an average of just over an inch every four years. Heading into the 1968 Olympics in Mexico City, the record stood at under 7 feet 2 inches.

Then an athlete by the name of Dick Fosbury came on the scene.

Fosbury ignored history and the conventional high jumping techniques. Instead, he threw himself over the bar backwards and head first while looking skyward, then landing on his back.

The result was stunning. He sailed over the bar at 7 feet 4 1/4 inches, shattering the Olympic record by more than two inches, shocking the crowd of 80,000 people and establishing the unorthodox style that was dubbed the "Fosbury Flop."[1] In the subsequent eight summer Olympics through the year 2000, 34 of the 36 Olympic medalists in the event used Fosbury's jumping technique.[2]

The high jump was still the same, simple event. It still involved a human body trying to thrust itself over a horizontal bar. But Fosbury's revolutionary style challenged the well-established techniques used by other Olympic athletes.

Fosbury could have played it safe and used the same old conventional techniques like everyone else. But if he had, chances are he would never have won his gold medal or achieved his lasting fame. Instead, Fosbury decided to *rethink* the high jump, unwilling to accept the plateau of achievement set by others. He broke from the pack and reached his goal by approaching the event in a new and different way.

As marketers, we can sometimes get in the same stale rut as Fosbury's high jumping contemporaries. Doing the "same old, same old" just is not working and to reach our goals, we need to break out with something new.

That is what *Rethink Your Marketing* can help you do. Just as Fosbury did with the high jump, you can break through and achieve new heights with your marketing. If your business is stuck and you just cannot seem to grow beyond your current plateau, *Rethink Your Marketing* offers multiple strategies for getting unstuck to propel revenue growth. If you are frustrated because you cannot move past the competition, *Rethink Your Marketing* provides you with proven methods for blindsiding the competition and achieving quantum leaps in your marketing results.

Do you have a great product or service? Is your staff committed? Do you have happy customers? You may have all of these, but sorry, this typically is not enough to generate rapid growth. Even with all of these positives, you may still feel like you are going around in circles without the results to show for your efforts.

It is maddening, right? What is a company to do?

Often, businesses in this position look to their marketing program and tend to do one of three things:

- Copy what the competition is doing.
- Do what the media is hyping at the moment.
- Do what they have done in the past.

Unfortunately, these are precisely the wrong things to do and typically end in failure and more frustration.

If you are facing this dilemma when it comes to your marketing efforts, take heart. There is a way out, but it means changing the way you look at your marketing. *Rethink Your Marketing* is a business guide that teaches you how to get unstuck. This book:

- Demonstrates how to increase business success and

drive significant growth – by rethinking your approach to marketing from seven distinct angles.

- Enables you to cut through all the noise to identify the true sources of your revenue growth.
- Offers many examples of companies of all sizes that have changed course in order to achieve amazing results.

Rethink Your Marketing identifies seven key strategies for you to jumpstart your growth engine. The good news is that most businesses will not have to go through all seven. In some cases, a mix of methods will be effective. For others, merely focusing on just one of the seven strategies will be enough to get you where you need to go. But one thing is clear: virtually every company will find at least one of these strategies to help jumpstart its marketing transformation.

So, are you tired of treading water? Are you looking for a way for your business to break out and reach its full potential? By using one or more of the seven strategies for rethinking your marketing, you will uncover ways to transform your marketing results.

It is time for you to take action. It is time for you to *Rethink Your Marketing*.

1

RETHINK YOUR AUDIENCE

When David Hauser and Siamak Taghaddos founded the virtual phone systems provider Grasshopper, they started out by targeting both small businesses and entrepreneurs. Sounds logical, right? Both groups require phone systems. With the increase in remote workers and distributed teams, it is clear why they wanted to reach both audiences.

However, over time, the company realized that entrepreneurs were far more profitable for Grasshopper than small businesses, as entrepreneurs stayed with the service longer and required less tech support. Entrepreneurs wear many hats, and so when they find a service that works it makes sense for them to stick with it and focus their energies elsewhere.

Given its insight into the value of entrepreneurs as an audience segment, Grasshopper started A/B testing its marketing messaging and found the entrepreneurial message converted better. For example, the company tested Hauser's and Taghaddos' own entrepreneurial story on the company's home page. The message resonated and site conversions increased.

Having identified the company's most prized segment, Grasshopper could now focus all of its effort, time, and resources on entrepreneurs, further strengthening its positioning against competitors. All of Grasshopper's marketing efforts became hyper-targeted at entrepreneurs, and included, among other things, giving away 10,000 complimentary copies of Mark Cuban's book *How to Win at the Sport of Business* to its customers.[1]

Gaining better marketing results was only one of many benefits Grasshopper realized by better defining its audience. Grasshopper was able to uncover, roll out, and profit from additional services that entrepreneurs found valuable. In addition, entrepreneurs were satisfied with a self-service model, enabling Grasshopper to automate the process, significantly slashing costs.

To date, according to its website, Grasshopper has serviced more than 300,000 customers. Clearly, its audience segmentation strategy worked and enabled the company to grow exponentially.

It would have been easy for Grasshopper to continue targeting both entrepreneurs and SMB's. By rethinking its audience, though, Grasshopper found the "sweet spot" of its customer base and unleashed unprecedented revenue growth.

Grasshopper learned the value of defining and targeting its most highly valued audience segment and as a result, a company that started out as just two guys with a dream became the dominant player in the phone systems market for entrepreneurs.

By changing its strategy and focusing on a narrower audience, Grasshopper grew to $30 million in revenue and was ultimately acquired by Citrix for approximately $165 million in cash plus stock.² That is the value of rethinking your audience!

It Takes Guts To Rethink Your Audience

The best place to start when rethinking your marketing is with your target audience. After all, these are the people who you want to find your offerings so valuable that they are willing to pay you instead of your competitors.

Over time, a company can slowly become disconnected from its target audiences. This is a natural process that occurs as the company gets larger, processes ossify, and the firm falls back on the status quo to survive. Many companies simply identify their largest (or easiest to acquire and manage) customers as their "ideal" target audience. This is a reactive approach to thinking about audiences.

Rethinking your audience can be difficult and requires not only detailed data analysis, but also some serious soul-searching. Committing to a change and ending your marketing efforts to certain audience segments is even harder. It takes courage. It takes will. It takes an iron stomach as you explore what works and what does not with your narrower audience. But the rewards for your efforts can be eye-popping!

Audience Segmentation As A Growth Driver

Defining your audience can drive growth, or it can cause stagnation if not handled properly. It is important to determine your value to different types of customers and prospects, and then to focus like crazy to uniquely serve these specific businesses or individuals.

This is called audience segmentation. The more keenly you are able to define your audience segments, the easier your marketing will be since you will have a crystal clear picture of the people to whom you are communicating. Audience segmentation makes your customer research easier. It makes your persona-building easier. It makes your distribution channel decisions easier. It makes your messaging easier. It makes your lead generation easier. In other words, audience segmentation works like a laser beam, focusing you more directly on your ideal prospects and enabling you to more powerfully move them to action.

If your marketing targets small businesses, should you focus on specific verticals, company sizes, or geographies? Or should you focus on job titles? Even if you are targeting a niche as narrow as law firms, for example, you may have very distinct audience segments such as partners vs. associates vs. paralegals vs. marketing directors vs. administrative personnel.

For example, MyCase is a law practice management system that targets partners. The software includes modules for case and matter organization, billing, and secure client communication. FastCase is another software product for law firms, but is a package that many paralegals find useful for case research. Lexicata is a CRM software solution for law firms especially of interest to marketing directors. All three software offerings target law firms, but each has a specific focus tailored to different roles and job functions inside the firm.

In theory, audience segmentation is simple, but can be difficult in practice. Many companies lose focus and attempt to be all things to all prospective customers. How many times have you agreed to do business with an audience or company that you knew deep down was a stretch and not really the right fit? It is time to be honest and dispel the notion that "any business is good business." It is time to get serious about your segmentation strategy.

Firing Clients To Unleash Growth

Sometimes, segmenting your audience for growth requires bold action. Such was the case with my first job in the United States after returning from four years at Panasonic in Tokyo.

After arriving back in the U.S., I joined a Japanese translation agency in the Boston area. When I joined the agency, phones were ringing off the hook. Normally a good thing, right? What I soon realized, however, was that the majority of the calls were for business card translations or other small projects. The avalanche of tiny orders was dragging the company down and preventing revenue growth. Although everyone was "busy," there was no strategy in place to intentionally drive growth.

That is when things got interesting.

Our team talked through the problem and decided the agency should focus exclusively on the software industry, which typically generated projects in the $100,000-$300,000 price range. In addition, software companies released new upgrades continuously, providing an ongoing revenue stream.

Implementing the change meant making software localization our core business, instituting a minimum fee, and firing half of the agency's existing clients. Sure enough, the phone did not ring as much. Talk about needing an iron stomach!

But despite jettisoning half of the client roster, the company's revenue skyrocketed. By focusing exclusively on six-figure accounts, we were able to focus all of the company's resources on driving revenue growth. There was no more wasting time on small or unprofitable business. And the more software accounts we won, the easier it became to attract additional software accounts.

Within two years, the new model enabled the company to increase its annual revenue by 250 percent. A larger company in the industry then swooped in and acquired our fast-growing agency at a multiple of annual sales. This was a clear case of addition by subtraction – the result of effective audience segmentation.

As difficult as it may be, sometimes you simply must focus on your best clients and eliminate the rest. Trying to be too many things to too many audiences can bog your company down in a morass of seemingly endless busywork.

Differentiation becomes hard. Achieving clear expertise becomes more difficult. And providing superior service becomes nearly impossible. The more effectively you can center the entire organization on your ideal clients, the stronger you become in attracting similar clients. The result is more experience, success stories, and client testimonials to help you bring in the next new customer. The more you prune, the more you stand out to your ideal client and the more you grow as a result.

Too often, employees brag about how "busy" they are. And often, they are telling the truth – they are indeed busy. But being busy is not the same thing as being "busy driving growth." It is too easy to get bogged down in the day-to-day details of the job. Workers are heads-down on what is due that day. Executives lose focus and run around putting out fires. Leadership meanders, and the result is a rudderless ship.

The result? A company without a clear target audience. And a company without a clear target audience is a company that is busy being busy, with no clear revenue benefit.

Taking It A Step Further: Firing 60 Percent Of One's Clients To Unleash Growth

Imprivata is a security software company that early on targeted banks, financial institutions, and healthcare facilities. In 2009, after the financial sector collapse, the company's CEO, Omar Hussain, decided to focus solely on healthcare. What this meant, though, was letting go of 60 percent of the company's existing clients.

Although this might seem limiting, Imprivata's results mirrored those I had experienced at the translation company. It freed the company to focus all of its energy and resources on the specific needs of doctors, nurses, and healthcare providers.

Within three years, Imprivata's healthcare business increased by 40 percent, with sales in excess of $50 million.[3] Within six years, the company's sales surpassed $119 million. The company now has more than 2.8 million users in over 1,000 healthcare organizations. The company agreed to be acquired in July of 2016 at a 33 percent premium over its stock price, with the total value of the acquisition estimated at $544 million.[4] Not too shabby for a company that shed itself of 60 percent of its clients a few years earlier.

Turning To Micro-Targeting To Spark A Turnaround

A number of years ago I went to a marketing industry event near Boston and sat at a table with an empty chair. I wound up chatting with the guy to my left, and found him to be interesting and engaging. He turned out to be Mark Organ, the founder of a software company called Eloqua in Toronto.

Eloqua is a marketing automation and lead management software developer and provides another good example of the benefits of narrowing one's target audience to increase revenue. At one point, Eloqua was roughly a week away from bankruptcy, and Organ realized he needed to make some immediate changes. Rethinking Eloqua's target audience became central to turning the company around.

One of the keys to revitalizing Eloqua's sales was a new focus on micro-verticalization of the company's target audience. Eloqua identified niche markets with substantial revenue potential, and then aggressively targeted them.

The company looked for bright spots among the existing customer base, and found examples where its solution was differentiated and convincingly delivering substantial value. By using these existing successful customers as models, Eloqua was able to expedite the process by leapfrogging a good deal of research, planning, and debating. Looking at real use cases and actual feedback from these model customers allowed Eloqua to make progress fast, while building a more defined formula for broadening the effort to additional verticals over time. Several months after starting the micro-verticalization effort, Eloqua had a dedicated vertical team with a dedicated leader.

By marketing in this hyper-focused manner, Eloqua differentiated its offering from the competition and was able to raise prices. The new audience segmentation strategy worked and revenue climbed significantly.

"I think there's very little that's more important in the development of the startup than target-market identification and focus and being able to dominate a small niche," Organ explained in an interview in Entrepreneur magazine. "It's a great way to get profitable fast, grow fast, and . . . roll out of there to [adjacent markets] once you've started figuring something out that you can own."[5]

How did Organ ultimately fare? The company was growing so quickly that Oracle swooped in and acquired it for $871 million – a nice change in fortune for a company that was once a week away from bankruptcy.

Another example of a company that used micro-targeting to jumpstart growth was Knowledge Adventure, a developer of educational computer games for kids. Bill Gross, the Founder, had loved learning as a child. As a parent, he wanted to make sure that his son had the same love of learning as he grew up. With that in mind, Gross started Knowledge Adventure. The first products included Dinosaur Adventure, Science Adventure, and through a partnership with Buzz Aldrin, Space Adventure.

The problem was, the company was unsure if it could achieve its holiday sales goals.

There were 65 people at the company at the time, and Gross' brother suggested that each team member head out to an actual store to observe shoppers in action to see if that might lend a clue as to how to improve sales. Calling themselves the "Weekend Warriors," they visited the stores each weekend and would regroup and discuss their efforts each subsequent Monday morning.

What they noticed was that consumers in the stores would pick up one of the brand's products, read the box, but then place it right back on the shelf. Gross and the team had an epiphany. At the time, they were marketing the products broadly, as "fun for ages eight to 108." On the surface, this sounds like it would have produced a wide appeal among shoppers. The problem was, consumers did not know if it was the right product for their particular child. With the lack of certainty, they would inevitably return the product to where they had found it on the store shelf.

The team then decided to try a radical approach – creating a unique product for each grade.

They experimented with a product called JumpStart, and created a version for children in preschool, and a separate product for children in kindergarten. Immediately, sales for these products were 20X to 50X higher than Knowledge Adventure's other products, according to Gross.

The company learned that by micro-targeting by grade, parents not only bought the product for their particular child's grade, but also for the next grade to give their child a leg up. Parents of a three year-old, for example, were buying the kindergarten version and even the eventual first grade version of the product. The company ultimately created a version for toddlers as well as each grade level up through sixth grade.

Prior to the audience targeting pivot, Knowledge Adventure had been selling tens of thousands of units of its products. After the switch to micro-targeting, it sold 20 million units.[6]

Sometimes, you have a good product but just need to rethink your audience targeting in a way that speaks directly to very narrow segments within the market. This one change can make all the difference.

From Bankruptcy To Fast Growth

After Popcorn Palace, maker of flavored gourmet popcorn went bankrupt, Timothy Heitmann acquired the company's name and recipes. The unique popcorn flavors like Cookies & Dream, Chicago Chic, and Jalapeno were clearly stronger than the company's financials.

At first, Heitmann tried numerous ways to sell the popcorn, including ecommerce, wholesale, QVC, and big box retailers. Then one day he received a letter from a boy who used the popcorn to raise money for his school band.

Epiphany! Heitmann rethought his audience and decided that instead of trying to sell to individuals through a maze of distribution channels, Popcorn Palace would target schools and organizations looking to raise funds.

The result? Popcorn Palace has made the Inc. 5,000 list of fastest growing private companies in the U.S. a whopping 10 times.

Heitmann hesitantly tried to accommodate a few remaining big-box clients. However, the product sat on shelves for long periods of time, losing its freshness. So, although the short-term influx of revenue was attractive, it compromised the quality of the product and did not strategically align to Popcorn Palace's true audience. The experience sealed Heitmann's decision to stick to its new target audience.

Today, Popcorn Palace focuses its sales on fundraising organizations, ecommerce and corporate gift accounts. Popcorn Palace is a tasty example of growth through focusing on the right audience segments.[7]

How The King Of The Bagel Baskets Redefined Its Destiny

These examples demonstrate how focusing on narrower audience segments is certainly one formula for unleashing revenue growth. Another method of driving revenue growth by rethinking one's audience is to simply target a completely different audience.

In 1998, Marlin Steel Wire Products was "king of the bagel baskets." As demand for bagels declined and half-priced foreign basket imports flooded the market, Marlin found itself in a world of pain. Even without the drop in demand or increase in foreign competition, the market for bagel shops was always going to be limited for Marlin. Having dominated the market with $800,000 in annual revenue, they were a big fish in a very small pond. Marlin faced an uphill battle to drive meaningful growth.

With this backdrop, Drew Greenblatt bought Marlin and rethought its audience. Greenblatt started targeting businesses in the aerospace, defense, medical, and automotive industries, where the market is many times larger – factories outnumber bagel shops in the United States by 100X – and buyers are comparatively price-insensitive.

Greenblatt's first sales call with a Boeing engineer revealed that the requested specifications were much more stringent than any bagel shop had ever required. What struck Greenblatt, though, was that even though he quoted the engineer a price that was double the standard price per basket, the engineer did not flinch and simply asked how quickly he could receive the shipment. That is when Greenblatt realized Marlin was no longer in the steel wire basket business and had moved into the engineering and precision business.[8]

As a result, Greenblatt went all-in targeting these new industries and annual revenue has grown 10X since he rethought its audience.[9] In addition to Boeing, clients now include NASA, Honda, Toyota, Delta Air Lines, and General Electric according to the company's website. Sometimes, no matter what you do, you are facing a limited market and the only way to drive revenue growth is to shift target markets altogether.

Moving To A New Market Segment With A Stronger Value Proposition

Sometimes you can target a new vertical in order to propel growth like Marlin Steel Wire Products did. You can also seek out market segments that provide higher value propositions.

iMotions is the developer of a biometric research platform that lets researchers integrate best-in-class biosensors, eye tracking, facial expression analysis, electroencephalogram (EEG), galvanic skin response (GSR), electromyography (EMG), Electrocardiogram (ECG), and surveys in one unified software platform. This emotion-detection technology provides clearer, more accurate information for iMotions clients, a quantum leap from traditional focus groups.

After initially targeting marketing agencies, iMotions found that its platform was actually a better fit elsewhere.

"We had traditionally focused on marketing agencies, but have moved into the academic segment," CEO Peter Hartzbech explained. "The academic segment has proven to be more mature, and we have had an even better product market fit. We have a stronger value proposition in this segment, and it is scalable and predictable. Today this is our primary segment."

iMotions did not stop at just changing industry verticals, either, narrowing its approach to identify individuals within target organizations.

"With the constantly improving ease of use of the iMotions software platform it has been much easier for people to get started," Hartzbech stated. "This has enabled us to successfully onboard more beginner type personas who hadn't been doing biometric research previously. Tapping into that segment has increased our target audience by at least 5X and enables us to continue our high growth."

Bypassing The Traditional Buyer To Fuel $826.9 Million In Annual Revenue

Marlin Steel Wire Products and iMotions looked to different target industries to boost growth. Another way to rethink your target audience is to look to different departments within your existing target industries. That is the approach taken by Tableau Software, developers of business intelligence and data visualization solutions.

Tableau is more powerful than Microsoft Excel, and easier to use than business intelligence products from IBM, SAP, and Oracle. The software helps business people make sense of their data, enabling them to ask better questions, uncover trends, identify opportunities, and make data-based decisions. It further empowers them to share insights in a highly visual, stunning, and easy-to-interpret way, benefiting everyone in the organization.

When the company started, however, sales did not come easily. In the early days, co-founder Christian Chabot drove around Silicon Valley in his beat-up Geo Prizm trying to get IT departments interested in the software only to continually run into dead ends. Back then, the standard way of dealing with data was for IT departments to respond to business users' requests, and configure reports accordingly. The IT department was the gateway into the corporation for data-based software companies. Unfortunately for Chabot, the IT folks just were not that interested in his software.

Chabot rethought his target audience. Clearly, he was getting nowhere with the IT gatekeepers, yet he knew there was real value for organizations in what Tableau was offering. So, he pivoted. Instead of approaching IT departments, he tried something that was heretical – and potentially suicidal for a sales team. He went directly to the business users.

That change made all the difference in the world. IT resources historically do not care if a report looks "pretty" or what font is included in a chart, but business users and marketers care about that stuff. A lot! It transforms the data from a sea of numbers into visuals that tell a story and reveal insights.

Marketers and business users had always been underwhelmed with the types of reporting coming out of IT. Tableau offered a new and exciting visual experience with an ease-of-use that was a dream come true for many marketers.

Now, a wide variety of organizations make use of visualization software. Major league baseball teams use the software to analyze ticket sales in near real-time and monitor how beer sales are impacting the bottom line. Presenting complex data sets in this way enables the backend staff to make real-time operational decisions that result in a more profitable organization.

By changing its target audience, Tableau unleashed massive growth. The software company grew by more than 1,900% over the past six years, and now boasts more than 54,000 customers in its portfolio. Tableau achieved annual revenue of $826.9 million in 2016, a 27 percent increase over the prior year.[10]

Tableau's strategy of bypassing IT in the sales process also paved the way for many other software companies such as Box and Slack to use a similar approach.

Expanding Geographically For 20X Growth

ZenPayroll was founded in 2012 and within three years grew into a $1 billion company. Not too shabby.

What was the key to its meteoric growth? Certainly, its cloud-based solution featured an attractive user interface. And targeting the small business market turned out to be a fortuitous decision. But geography also played a critical role.

When ZenPayroll started, it delivered its payroll services to clients only in its local area in California. From there, it expanded outward and by 2013 it was processing approximately $100 million with 100 clients. By 2015 the company (which changed its name to Gusto) was doing business in all 50 states, boasting 20,000 clients – a remarkable 20X increase over two years.[11] That same year the company closed a $60 million Series B round of funding, raising the value of the company to $1 billion. Had Gusto maintained its geographical focus on California, that type of growth would not have been possible.

Often, companies concentrate on the same geographic area in which they have historically been doing business. However, branching out geographically can sometimes be one of the simplest methods to juice your revenue. You already have your products, services, processes, and customer support team in place. It is relatively easy to replicate this infrastructure for the same types of customers in a different location.

Bain & Company conducted a five-year study of specific growth-driving moves by 1,850 companies to determine how successful companies achieve sustainable, profitable growth. The research revealed that companies realize their most ongoing, profitable growth when they push out the boundaries of their core business into an adjacent space including adjacent geography. The study also found that successful growth companies consistently develop a formula for expanding those boundaries in predictable, repeatable ways.[12]

Gusto could have expanded across the West. They could have crossed over into the Midwest. Instead, they went national, and ultimately even expanded internationally.

Are you everywhere your business should be today?

I had a similar experience when a British company hired me to set up its first U.S. office and establish a foothold in the U.S. market. By focusing on geographic expansion with the same operational capacity and processes, we more than tripled the company's revenue within two years. Some of the multi-billion dollar companies I was able to secure as clients included IBM, Bose, Hewlett-Packard, and CA.

Was it hard work? Yes, absolutely. However, from a strategic perspective, this was one of the most efficient, frictionless methods for generating accelerated revenue growth.

WP Engine is another example of a company using geographic expansion to fuel rapid revenue growth. The company is a website hosting platform for WordPress, the most popular content management system (CMS), now powering roughly 26 percent of businesses on the web. WP Engine boasts the largest group of WordPress developers in the world.

"Geographically, we have clients in over 1,363 countries – nearly 70 percent of the world," Mary Ellen Dugan, CMO at WP Engine told me. "In fact, 5 percent of the entire online world visits at least one WP Engine-hosted property, every single day. It is amazing to see the growth of WordPress in all countries. Given our current footprint, we are confident we can serve more geographic clients."

Dugan went on to highlight the need for cultural respect in refining one's approach to geographic expansion in order to make the approach successful.

Has the strategy worked in fueling growth for WP Engine? Actually, that would be an understatement. WP Engine recently announced that it has surpassed 60,000 customers, 50 percent growth from the just under 40,000 a year ago.

Another good example of growth through geographic expansion comes from Robert Herjavec, a Canadian businessperson and investor, seen as one of the sharks on ABC's popular TV show Shark Tank. Before joining Shark Tank, The Herjavec Group focused on the Canadian market for its enterprise security software. This helped the company grow to $155 million within 10 years. Since then, the company has expanded into the United States and the United Kingdom, all part of a three-year, $250 million expansion plan.

"One of the things I'm most proud of is that less than two years ago, one percent of our sales were outside of Canada. Last year, 26 percent were, and this year, 40 percent will be," Herjavec explained in an Inc. article. "Now I look back and say, 'Why didn't we do this sooner?' Before we opened our New York office, and others internationally, I asked other company founders I met who export either products or services, 'What's the key? What is the first thing you did?' They all said, 'We showed up. That's how you start.' So now, as a result, Herjavec Group doesn't look at the Canadian market or the U.S. market. We look at a global market. Since cybersecurity is in so much demand, we also think, 'Someone is going to dominate the world – why can't that be us?'"[13]

Beautifully said.

Expanding Demographics To Create A Multi-billion Dollar Business

Expanding geographically is certainly one way to propel revenue growth, but you can also increase sales through demographic growth. On February 4, 2004, there was a kid at Harvard who decided to launch a social networking site for students at his school. Within 24 hours, between 1,200 to 1,500 students signed up for the service. Within a month, more than half of the nearly 20,000 registered students had joined. The site, of course, was "Thefacebook.com," with the name later changed to Facebook after the company spent $200,000 for the domain Facebook.com.[14]

The service was then opened up to students at Stanford, Columbia, and Yale. After that, the other Ivy League schools and some Boston area schools joined in followed quickly by many other colleges and universities. In September of 2005, a high school version of the social network was created. In December of that year, Facebook had 2,000 colleges and 25,000 high schools on board. In September of 2006, the service opened up to anyone 13 years old or older with a valid email address. Later, the company launched Business Pages for companies.

Had Facebook continued to limit its focus to Harvard, or to universities in general, or to only universities and high schools, it would have severely stunted its growth and would be a shadow of the company that it is today. Instead, Facebook incrementally expanded its audience to include more groups. This is another validation of the Bain & Company study that found that sustained, profitable growth comes when a company pushes out the boundaries of its core business and then develops a formula for consistently expanding those boundaries in predictable, repeatable ways.

Facebook's IPO raised approximately $16 billion, earning it the distinction of the third largest in U.S. history. Revenue for the full year in 2016 was close to $27 billion.[15] At the time of this writing, Facebook's website reported that it had 1.28 billion daily active users and offices in most major cities in the world.

What started as a website for students at a single university has become a business juggernaut. This is the power of rethinking your audience through incremental expansion.

Discovering A New Path With A Crazy Broad Audience

Basecamp is a successful project management software company spread across 32 cities around the world – quite a leap from its modest beginnings in 1999 when Jason Fried and three others started a web design firm called 37Signals. Its model was helping companies like Panera and Shopping.com build and redesign their corporate websites.

Website projects involve seemingly endless details like gathering existing design assets, brand style guides, creative assets, fonts, copy, and web analytics account logins. You need to define a website strategy, establish key performance indicators (KPIs), and develop conversion funnels. You must optimize the site for search engines across technical issues, content, and even offsite considerations. You need to think through the user experience (UX) and interactivity. You need to incorporate new designs that are aligned to the brand strategy. You need to manage multiple client reviews. And nowadays, you also need to build responsively, enabling the site to be usable on multiple devices with an array of screen dimensions.

How did the folks at 37Signals manage this chaos? Through email. Is email meant to manage large, long-term projects? No. Is email meant to be a communication, file management, and scheduling tool for teams? No. Project management by email leads to version control problems, difficulty in finding key pieces of information, people being left out of key communications, confusion as to who is doing what, lack of an audit trail, and no real way to communicate status and next steps.

So, you can imagine the frustration that the 37Signals employees were feeling as they tried to wrangle with all of the elements of a website project using email. They tried various project management tools, but found them to be overly complex and difficult to use, and so they inevitably reverted back to email.

With frustration mounting, the team decided to build its own simple project management application. The solution it developed solved many problems and projects began to run smoother, making the team at 37Signals much happier. Clients appreciated the clearer communications and better organization of projects and began to ask about the new tool the agency was using that helped achieve this more seamless process. They wanted to use it for their own in-house projects.

On February 5, 2004, 37Signals released its tool – Basecamp – to the world. It made the announcement in the company blog and within a month had landed almost a hundred paying customers. Within a year, Basecamp was driving more revenue than web design services for 37Signals.

That was the "A-Ha!" moment when 37Signals realized it was in the wrong business. It changed the name of the company to Basecamp, reflecting a core focus on the project management solution and went all-in on the software business.

Instead of being limited to an audience of only marketing departments, Basecamp was now selling to a wide range of departments and people – essentially anyone in need of managing projects. Millions of users signed up.

Within ten years of the launch, Basecamp user volume reached nearly 15 million with thousands of additional companies signing up every week. Basecamp now boasts over 100,000 companies as paying customers, is debt-free, and has been profitable every year since it launched.

Although Basecamp originally started out by focusing on marketing departments, it ultimately pivoted to target any organization with projects – an audience of most organizations on the planet. The result has been spectacular growth and success.

How Fitbit Used A Platform To Scale Its Audience Reach

One more way to unleash growth is to identify a "platform" to help you reach your audience in much greater scale. Fitbit is a case in point.

Fitbit is the largest seller of wearable activity trackers by shipments. It recorded $2.17 billion in annual revenue in 2016, which represented growth of more than 191 percent over the same period two years prior.[16] Yet, lurking beneath those robust numbers is a minefield of well-funded competitors such as Apple and Samsung attempting to eat away at Fitbit's market share.

Going head to head with technology behemoths is usually not the most strategically astute decision. Industry giants have resources far greater than anything Fitbit could even dream of and can easily outspend the company. To fend off this threat and continue its growth trajectory, Fitbit needed to rethink its audience.

According to Forbes, approximately 80 percent of US employers have corporate wellness programs such as subsidizing gym memberships. Companies spend an average of $693 per employee in such programs, a figure that has been growing over the years.[17] By targeting this market, Fitbit can make one sale to a corporation and in effect reach hundreds or thousands of employees.

Fitbit dove into the corporate wellness market with gusto and now has thousands of employers as customers, with certain organizations ordering six-figures worth of devices. Margins are better and Fitbit faces fewer competitors in this part of the market. The more corporate wellness clients it signs up, the healthier Fitbit gets.

As substantial an achievement this has been, it is actually only the beginning for Fitbit. There are even more possibilities for tracking an employee's health that Fitbit can leverage. In the future, devices will likely become even more useful as they become specially customized for specific health conditions. Employers will be able to use Fitbit's metrics to demonstrate higher levels of staff activity to insurance providers and parlay that into lower premiums.

This platform has the potential to drive Fitbit's growth for years to come as more employers recognize the value of keeping their workers healthy. As they begin realizing financial benefits – like lower insurance premiums – they will begin asking Fitbit for devices that measure additional health points. It is a cyclical win-win-win.

Identifying platforms that help accelerate your reach to a target audience can be instrumental to your growth, but it does change your customer personas. With corporate wellness programs, Fitbit needed to market to human resource individuals inside of corporations administering or starting such programs. This is quite a stretch from the health-conscious consumer market it concurrently targets.

Platforms are accelerators that help you expand your reach exponentially. It is a theme we will revisit throughout this book.

Strategically Adding A New Audience Segment

L'Oréal is clearly a successful brand. Yet even brands with a healthy business can look to audience segmentation to spark new growth.

Historically, the company had primarily highlighted Caucasian women in its advertising, with only an occasional nod to Latinos and African Americans. Due to this imbalanced approach, walking into a department store's beauty section had been off-putting to many women with a variety of skin tones. Parent company Lancôme finally woke up in 2014 and realized it was underserving women of color.

In the U.S., the multicultural beauty market is outpacing the overall industry, according to research firm Kline & Co. WWD reports that African-American women spend $7.5 billion annually on beauty products, and pay 80 percent more on cosmetics and 2X more on skin care products than the market average.[18]

Lancôme moved to place diversity and globalization at the center of its strategy with a mission of "Beauty for All." It appointed Kenyan actress Lupita Nyong'o as its first black spokesperson in 2014. L'Oréal is now aggressively looking at markets beyond the U.S. and Europe and is investing in products with a diverse set of skin tones to appeal to a broader range of women. As part of this new strategy, the company has opened L'Oreal's Women of Color Lab tasked with creating groundbreaking new products for multicultural women.

Initial indications are that the broader, more diverse, and inclusive approach is having positive results. L'Oréal did the right thing by expanding its offering and its financials reaffirm the strategy. It reported sales increases over the past few years and overall annual sales of more than $29 billion and 17.6 percent profits in 2016.[19]

Building A Multi-billion Dollar Empire Like A Superhero

Marvel as a brand could not be further removed from L'Oréal – cosmetics and beauty vs. superheroes and adrenaline-filled action movies. Yet it approached expanding its business using audience segmentation in a very similar way.

Marvel had traditionally focused on kids. Later, it realized that adults (like me...) are just kids who never grew up and can love comic books and superhero stories as much as any child. They also knew that this new target audience could spend much more money.

Growing up, I loved Batman on TV, as well as Superman, The Hulk, and The Fantastic Four comic books. For a long-time, I had a voracious appetite for anything related to superheroes and had an up-and-close view of Marvel's properties. At the time, though, many adults dismissed comics as a waste of time.

Although Marvel dominated the comic book universe for decades, it hit a brick wall in the 1990's. Between 1993 and 1996, the comic book and trading card industry tanked and as a result, Marvel actually went broke. Coming out of bankruptcy, the company suffered enormous internal turmoil during a restructuring.

Finally, at the end of 1998, Marvel set along a new path based on a new strategy. Under newly appointed CEO Joseph Calamari, who had overseen Marvel in the 80's, Marvel started targeting adults along with kids with a new focus on the movie business. The company never looked back.

The X-Men movie, released in 2000, and a series of Spider-Man films, initiated in 2002, were mega blockbusters. X-Men ultimately earned $300 million worldwide, while the first of Sam Raimi's trilogy of Spider-Man movies brought in $100 million in its opening weekend alone. Since then, Spider-Man films have grossed over $3.9 billion. The initial Iron Man movie grossed $585 million worldwide.

Marvel has subsequently released an avalanche of movies leveraging the platforms of each individual brand, concurrently propelling growth in multiple directions. For example, Iron Man was followed by Iron Man 2 and Iron Man 3. These were paired with a series of Captain America and Thor movies. Marvel released the initial The Avengers movie in 2012 and another in 2015, and there is a third movie in the series also scheduled to be released. Marvel extended the brand again with the release of Ant-Man in 2015.

Today, X-Men, Spider-Man, Iron Man, and The Avengers are each billion-dollar franchises. Since the release of the first Iron Man film in 2009, Marvel's worldwide movies have grossed over $10 billion.

A significant side benefit has been the resuscitation of the comic book industry. Sales of comic books and graphic novels surpassed $1 billion overall in 2015[20], a nearly four-fold jump over $265 million fifteen years earlier.[21]

It doesn't take super powers to see that audience segmentation can make a world of a difference. Marvel had crashed and gone bankrupt. But by rethinking its audience and expanding its target market to include adults, it was able to not only survive, but to eventually grow into one of the strongest entertainment brands in the world.

A Stylish 10X Increase In Sales

I remember in elementary school wearing Converse Chuck Taylor All Star sneakers (which is what we called them in those days). It was the classic look. The vintage rubber toecap. The canvas. The color-contrasting sidewall. At that time, Chuck Taylors were not retro. They were it. They were the shoes to wear. I wanted to be a professional athlete like many other boys my age, and Converse represented athletics. Many pro athletes wore Converse shoes and would not have considered any other brand back then.

Converse was founded in 1908 and from the beginning ruled the athletic shoe market until the 1970s. That is when Nike and Adidas burst into the market, and using superior marketing machines, muscled Converse off the playing court and into bankruptcy court. Nike and Adidas were cool. Converse felt old, tired, and outdated. Converse lost its luster, and there was no compelling reason for anyone to want to wear the product anymore.

Two years after bankruptcy in July of 2003, Nike swooped in to acquire the iconic brand, eyeing a new market opportunity. Nike is known as one of the best marketing organizations on the planet. From "Just Do It" to "Unlimited You," the company continually pumps out exceptional marketing campaigns. It applied its Nike magic to the Converse brand and engineered a brilliant turnaround.

How did Nike do it? It rethought Converse's target audience.

Nike did the unimaginable. The Converse brand that had catered to athletes for close to a century, now turned its back on the sports world. Instead of targeting athletes, it began to target individuals looking for style and fashion. The strategy was for Converse to appeal to those wishing to look great at school or for a hip night out on the town.

The re-invented Converse brand began by partnering with musicians. It opened Rubber Tracks, a recording studio for emerging artists in Brooklyn, Boston, and Brazil, and collaborated with world-renowned producers and sound engineers in a curated set of music studios around the world. In total, artists have spent more than 11,000 hours in Rubber Tracks studios recording new music. Converse has taken the music theme even further, hosting concerts that feature Rubber Tracks artists.

Converse's annual sales were $205 million when Nike acquired the company. Today, Converse is a nearly $2 billion brand, a 10X increase in annual sales.[22] As equally important as the financial results, Converse has now bonded with a new, younger generation, as evidenced by its 39 million+ followers on Facebook, one of the top 100 followed pages ahead of such giants as Starbucks and Pepsi.

Just one more shining example of the power of rethinking your audience.

Chapter Summary

Is your current audience your ideal audience, or is it instead just what has evolved over time? Is it time to reconsider your audience and become more strategic in your targeting? There is a chance that by going narrower or broader in focus, or by changing your geographic or demographic focus, you can increase revenue even without changing your product or service.

Rethinking your target audience can expand your reach or lead you to a better product fit. Rethinking your audience is a powerful way to unleash revenue growth.

- Is your current target audience your ideal audience?
- How can you become more laser-focused within your target audience to identify segments on a more granular basis?
- Are there audience segments that you can eliminate from your targeting altogether to strengthen your ability to dominate in a specific area?
- What other industries, departments, or titles have a need for your products or services?
- Into which regions can you expand geographically?
- How can you incrementally add new demographics to your target audience?
- What are potential "platforms" to leverage in producing more scalability in your market traction?

2

RETHINK HOW THEY THINK

"$20K for a watch?? Did @Verizon price this?!"

"Yikes @ATT! Terrible Q3 results! Could explain the focus on buying another company! Any other diversion tactics!?"

"$600M in Duopoly overage profits! Disgusting."

Are these the Tweets of a crazed lunatic who likes to criticize telecom companies? Well, yes and no. He acts like he is insane and curses like a sailor. But he is a genius in certain ways, too. And he is always, always, always marketing.

I am talking about John Legere, the CEO of T-Mobile US. He completely rethought T-Mobile's marketing, and ever since he has been unleashing a torrent of messages that gets his millions of Twitter followers fired up and T-Mobile's revenue flowing. As CEO, he enabled T-Mobile to double its customers in four years, growing the business into the third largest and the fastest growing mobile carrier in the U.S.

What in the world is going on?

When Legere joined T-Mobile, the company was struggling to survive. It was badly behind Verizon, AT&T, and Sprint. Legere repositioned the company as the "Un-carrier", as the underdog who was hellbent on destroying all the anti-consumer, soul-sucking practices of the mobile industry at that time. He viewed the charges for overages, the outrageous cancellation fees, and the heartless call centers as the bane of the industry. He vowed to change it all, and he has been following through.

T-Mobile was the first U.S. carrier to eliminate two-year contracts and to offer "no contract" plans, all as part of the Un-carrier manifesto geared to making T-Mobile the opposite of the other wireless providers in the industry.

Not only does Legere go on tirades against competitors, he is also on social media around the clock answering customers' tweets directly. He is so loved and popular that Twitter created an emoji specifically for him – only the second person to ever be so honored. His closet full of magenta t-shirts with a large T-Mobile "T" and black sport coats enables him to wear T-Mobile colors every day of the week.

Why has Legere been so successful at turning around T-Mobile? Because he voices what we all feel. He knows that people are outraged at how they have been treated by wireless carriers, and he openly says what we are all thinking. He points out the obvious. He screams about it. He highlights when something is as asinine as it sounds. That level of authenticity has endeared him to millions.

By being so vocal about issues that nearly all wireless consumers were feeling, he evoked an emotional response from his audience. Even if you did not like his potty mouth, you had to like his fearlessness in calling out the industry. And as a marketer, you had to like how he fired up his target audience.

Understanding How They Think

What has made John Legere so successful with his aggressive marketing approach? Much of it can be explained by the way the human brain operates and the way people think.

Do you believe that your audience members are in full control when they are considering making a purchase? Do you feel that they are highly rational in thinking through purchase decisions? Do you think they read every word of your website, newsletter, and marketing collateral and process each word in a logical fashion?

Think again.

According to Nielsen, 90 percent of purchase decisions are made by the subconscious mind. (Gerald Zaltman, Emeritus Professor at Harvard Business School, actually places this figure at 95 percent.) Whereas 11 million bits of sensory information are processed subconsciously every second, less than 100 bits are processed by the conscious brain. As humans, we are dominated by the subconscious. Yet many marketers ignore this and focus their efforts on getting people to change their conscious minds.

There are approximately 100 billion neurons in the human brain. These neurons create trillions of electrical or chemical connections through synapses that help formulate thought, reasoning, and memory. PhD students from Carnegie Mellon and University of California, Berkeley found that the human brain is up to 30 times more powerful than the world's most powerful supercomputer.[1] Talk about power!

Considering the dominating influence that the human brain has on the purchasing decisions of a company's target audience, it is stunning how little focus marketers apply to neuroscience and psychology in the customer acquisition process at many companies.

It behooves you to leverage the power of the brain in attracting attention, building relationships, and spurring prospects to action. Legere certainly understands how people think and behave, and he crafted his style of communication accordingly.

You would think that understanding and leveraging such a powerful driver of human behavior would be a must for marketers – that it would be at the top of the list of all MBA programs' curriculum. Or that it would be a common topic of conversation at marketing planning meetings.

Yet that is just not the case, and this is one of the reasons why so many marketers have an incomplete view of their customers. It is one thing to be aware of a "customer need." It is quite another to understand *why* your audience feels the way they do, and what you need to do to engage with them at that subconscious level.

It is critical to understand the way your customers think, so you can then connect and engage them more deeply, communicate with them in a manner that resonates more directly, and drive them to the actions that matter most.

Our Three Brains

When talking about the human mind, it is important to look at its parts and talk about your customers' *three brains*: the old brain (R complex), the midbrain (limbic system), and the new brain (neocortex). Although each of the three serves a different function and even has a different cell structure, they work highly effectively as a team.

The old brain dates back about 450 million years ago and is focused on survival. In line with our primal instincts, it is constantly scanning the environment for any potential danger while also keeping an eye out for food. The old brain actually processes all incoming sensory data, most of it occurring at a subconscious level. What you see, what you hear, what you smell, what you touch is directed at the old brain. Back in the time of the cavemen and cavewomen, this type of survival mechanism was invaluable. Today, you likely face far fewer dangers, but the old brain still works to protect you from any threat that it detects, and often directs you to food to sustain you.

The midbrain, also called the mesencephalon, supports motor movement, such as for the eye, or auditory and visual processing, and it processes emotions and gut feelings.

The new brain, or neocortex, is the outer layer of the brain. The new brain is what enables humans to process language, have complex social interactions, play music, think through challenges, debate ideas, and plan for the future. The commonly held view by scientists is that it is the new brain, and especially the pre-frontal cortex where reasoning and logical thought take place, that makes us uniquely human. According to behavioral scientist Susan Weinschenk, though, it is actually that we have all three parts of the brain and their interaction with one another – their interconnectedness – that makes us uniquely human.

Here is something important to note about the old brain. It attempts to make decisions on its own, without the help of the other parts of the brain. This is because it is very fast at capturing and processing information. And then it makes a fight or flight decision. What is that coming at you? Is it something to embrace? Or should you freeze? Or should you flee? Your old brain makes these decisions for you instantaneously. The old brain forwards information to the new brain only when it is unable to make a decision on its own. Once the new brain receives new information, it takes more time than the old brain to process information.

From a marketing perspective, it is critical to understand that your decision-making and behavior are mostly processed subconsciously. Since you are only conscious of the new brain, it is natural for you to think it is driving your decisions. Yet the old brain and midbrain have an outsized impact on your actions, words, and behavior. Communicating with only the new brain limits the effectiveness of your marketing efforts.

It is time to rethink how your target audience actually thinks, how they actually decide what to do, and how they actually choose what to buy.

Why You Pay More For Similar Products

Do you like ice-cream? I sure do. I do not care what day of the week or what time of day it is, if you offered me ice-cream I would be your best friend.

Seriously, though, I have an ice-cream problem. I get excited just thinking about ice-cream (or just writing about it here...). And that got me thinking, why is it that one ice-cream brand can call itself premium and cost a few dollars a pint, while another can charge almost 5X as much.

We all know good ice-cream when we taste it. Yet it is rather easy to find ice-cream costing a few dollars that tastes like a million bucks.

eCreamery rotates 16 flavors daily at its store in Omaha,

Nebraska. It churns its flavors in a small batch process and hand packs flavors with care. It offers personalization of flavors as well as packaging.

It then charges you $69.99 for four pints (That is not a typo!), not including shipping costs for online orders. Wow!

I would argue it is this ridiculously high price that is garnering the brand such success. By charging 5X what others in the space are charging, it is a deviation that grabs your attention. You cannot help but take notice. You then immediately become intrigued, with your brain automatically trying to decipher why the ice-cream costs so much. The natural reaction is to think that the ingredients or the quality of the ice-cream is drastically greater than anything else on the market.

The social psychologist Robert Cialdini has explained that for "markets in which people are not completely sure of how to assess quality, they use price as a stand-in for quality."[1] In other words, raise your prices and your audience will often assume that you offer higher quality.

The strategy has certainly caught the attention of the press. The eCreamery brand has been highlighted by Oprah, The New York Times, Martha Stewart Living, Every Day with Rachael Ray, Esquire, ESPN, World News Tonight, and others. Warren Buffet and Paul McCartney have enjoyed ice-cream at the Omaha store. In the three months following the company's appearance on ABC TV's Shark Tank, eCreamery did $500,000 in sales. Not bad for a single-store ice-cream shop that charges 5X what you could essentially get down the street at the local supermarket.

If it were up to your new brain to decide whether the price of eCreamery ice-cream was logical, you would be at the supermarket looking at other brands in a flash. But because your brain operates mostly on a subconscious level, your brain lights up at the exceptionalism of the brand, making you actually yearn for the ice-cream. Not only is the price intriguing, piquing your curiosity, there is also a bit of exclusiveness and social proof that is influencing your decision. Add a story, add an emotional element, add branding that speaks to the subconscious, and like the effects of a magic pill, your pricing power immediately improves.

Significant Objects, an experiment conducted by writers Rob Walker and Joshua Glenn, provides proof of how adding stories increases a brand's ability to raise the price people are willing to pay for a product. Walker and Glenn purchased thrift-store, garage sale, and flea market objects, packaged them with a backstory and then tested their purchase price on eBay. On average, the purchase price of the items was $1.25. After being branded with a backstory and placed on eBay, the average resale price was a staggering $36.12.

For example, they bought a cat napkin ring for 50 cents and then sold it for $31. They purchased a felt mouse in a chef's hat for 50 cents and sold it for $62. They bought a wooden mallet for 33 cents and then sold it for $71. With a story, the buyer's brain changes and what the buyer sees as valuable changes along with it.

A wine experiment by Professors Hilke Plassmann, John O'Doherty, and Antonio Rangel at the California Institute of Technology and Baba Shiv at Stanford Graduate School of Business offers further evidence of the power of how pricing influences perceived value.[4] Theoretically, a person's perception of a product should reflect the make-up of the product and the state of the individual. In other words, in evaluating wine, the molecular composition of the drink should determine whether the person likes it or not. Simple as that.

Participants in the study were provided five glasses of Cabernet Sauvignon to taste under the pretense of studying the effect of degustation time on perceived flavors. In reality, they were given only three *different* wines, including the same wine priced at $10 and $90. Overall, the prices displayed were: $5 wine, $10 wine, $35 wine, $45 wine, $90 wine (the same wine as that labeled $10), and a neutral solution.

Subjects were asked to focus on the flavor of each wine. The study found that participants thought the $90 wine tasted better than the $10 wine, even though they were the same wine. Not only did the participants self-report these perceptions, but their bodies physically reacted to the prices differently as uncovered through functional MRI brain scanning. The medial orbitofrontal cortex (mOFC), an area of the brain thought to encode experiential pleasantness, reacted very differently when the subject was drinking $10 wine versus the $90 wine, indicating great pleasure – much more pleasure – when drinking the $90 wine, even though in reality it was the same wine.

The conclusion: if you are told a wine is more expensive, you will think it tastes better than a "less expensive" wine. And you will enjoy the experience more, both mentally and physically. *Even if both glasses contain the same exact wine.* Funny how the brain works.

In other words, if your marketing speaks to only the new brain, your marketing power will be limited. If you speak to the subconscious, you can exponentially increase your pricing power and profitability for the very same items.

The Power Of Emotions

You may assume your audience thinks logically when making decisions. Let us dig deeper to uncover what really drives them.

The neuroscientist Antonio Damasio conducted studies of people with damage to the area of the brain that triggers emotions.[5] Although they were functioning members of society, these individuals could not feel emotions. They could, however, remember dates, names, events, and details in the news.

What Damasio uncovered has massive ramifications for marketers. He found that these individuals who could not feel emotions found it extremely difficult to make any decisions. In other words, without emotions, they could not make the decision to purchase a product or service. This is because they did not feel strongly enough about one option versus another.

What this means for marketers is that if your marketing is not evoking an emotional response from your target audience, you are essentially making it extremely difficult for your prospective customers to make a purchase or engage with you. (It also means you are probably wasting your marketing budget.)

Historically, the scientific community spurned emotions and feelings as being insignificant. However, Damasio believed that the treatment of emotions and feelings in scientific circles was missing a deeper significance. He felt that not only were they important to study, but that they were interconnected with intellectual processes of the brain. In other words, emotions and feelings were integral to the act of reasoning. Your cognitive processes may be able to recognize a situation and conduct cold analysis of the facts, but it is your emotions that dictate what you feel is right or wrong, what you see as good or bad, what you should do versus what you should not do, and what you should or should not buy.

Your marketing can go on and on about how great your products, services, and people are. That should logically influence prospects' decisions. But at the end of the day, that is not what drives a person to action. Instead, it is their emotions.

Martin Lindstrom, author of the books *Buyology*, *Brand Sense*, and *Brandwashed*, conducted a study to explore the way our brains respond to a brand compared to a religion.[6] What he found was that our brain activity when viewing brand imagery such as from Apple and Harley-Davidson is highly similar to the brain activity when viewing religious imagery. When done right, branding is something that can bring you and your audience together in a very powerful way.

Nike is a company that went from selling shoes out of the trunk of a car to building a $32 billion marketing powerhouse. Nike's most iconic marketing campaign, "Just Do It", says absolutely nothing about the product. It says nothing about the technology. It says nothing about the design. What it does is evoke an emotive response. It speaks to the athlete inside you that wants to achieve greatness, even if you are not an athlete. Rather than being transactional, it is aspirational and motivational.

And that is precisely why it is so powerful.

In a Harvard Business Review interview, Phil Knight, co-founder and former CEO of Nike, said the following about emotional marketing: "From the beginning, we've tried to create an emotional tie with the consumer. Why do people get married—or do anything? Because of emotional ties. That's what builds long-term relationships with the consumer, and that's what our campaigns are about. That approach distinguishes us from a lot of other companies..."[7]

To this day I still remember being entranced and mesmerized when seeing the "Just Do It" ads on TV for the first time as a child, several decades ago. And now when I experience any of Nike's marketing, whether on its website, or in social media, or through events, I find it just as engaging.

Think about who you have fallen in love with in your life. It is based on your heart, not your mind. Even when it makes no logical sense, your heart wins the day and drives you to action. Similarly, people love brands and not only become attached to them, but emotionally associate themselves with them.

As Simon Sinek writes in *Start With Why*, many people who use Apple products are religiously devoted to them.[8] This is why it is not uncommon for customers to camp out overnight to be able to get their hands on the next iPhone or iPad. I once read about someone camping in front of an Apple Store for 10 days for an iPhone. Sinek points out that even if someone offered you a free phone of equal or better quality to an iPhone, many Apple devotees would not even consider it. They would still buy an iPhone, regardless of cost, over your better, free phone.

This is not rationality at work here. This is not the new brain in action here.

It is not a coincidence that Apple is also one of the most valuable companies on the planet. When you connect on a subconscious level with your customers, reason and logic take a backseat.

Why do people love Zappos? Is it because you can return shoes that do not fit or just do not feel right? Well, that is a small part of it. But it is the love Zappos fosters that makes all the difference.

Tony Hsieh, Zappos CEO, told a story about someone who called the Zappos customer support line inquiring about the location of the closest pizza shop. Rather than explaining to the person that Zappos does not sell pizza, the phone representative searched on his computer and provided the caller with the name and number of a local pizza place.

Jeffrey Hayzlett, former CMO at Kodak, Chairman of C-Suite Holdings, and bestselling author of *The Mirror Test, Running the Gauntlet,* and *Think Big, Act Bigger: The Rewards of Being Relentless*, explained to me how he evokes an emotional reaction in his audiences as follows: "By touching the core values of what the person represents. It's very clear that people react positively and negatively to any message no matter what it is. So your job is to find the message that pushes them one-way or the other. You can do that through constant understanding of your customer base and knowledge of what works and what doesn't.

"I think the key thing for great marketers is to create tension," says Hayzlett. "To create messages and campaigns that push people one way or the other. Just as much you want customers to say yes, you also want some to say no because it moves them to a decision point. This way you do not have to continually waste time trying to convince them to buy your product or service. That is why you see a lot of people going to humor or sex. Getting to a customer's core and moving them emotionally is what gives you greater value."

Emotion not only drives purchases, but also loyalty. Forrester Research concluded that emotions are the number one reason for customer loyalty in 17 of 18 industries that it studied.[9] It is not only product quality or customer support that drives loyalty.

After you have made the initial purchase, emotions play a major role in your decisions over the long haul.

If your business is stuck or in a rut, consider whether you are being too literal with your marketing. You may be focused on speaking to the wrong part of the brain.

The B2B Buyer Has Emotions, Too

Emotional marketing matters not only in the B2C (Business-to-Consumer) space, it is just as applicable to B2B (Business-to-Business) marketing.

The research report *From Promotion to Emotion: Connecting B2B Customers to Brands* by CEB and Google, found that purchase intent dips during the portion of the purchase funnel when messaging becomes less emotional.[10] The research found that brands achieve roughly twice the impact with a target audience when appealing to the personal value and emotional benefits to the buyer.

Google writes about the B2B experience: "Responsibility for a multi-million dollar software acquisition that goes bad can lead to poor business performance and even the loss of a job. The business customer won't buy unless there is a substantial emotional connection to help overcome this risk."

Google Senior VP of Global Marketing, Lorraine Twohill, states, "If we don't make you cry, we fail. It's about emotion."[11]

Twohill is not alone in expressing this sentiment. Multiple studies point to emotional marketing as more effective than other forms of marketing (e.g., product-focused marketing). Based on an analysis of 1,400 successful ad campaigns, the book *Brand Immortality* by Hamish Pringle and Peter Field reveals that advertising campaigns focused on emotional content performed approximately twice as well (31 percent vs. 16 percent) as those with only rational content.[12]

Findings from a 2015 Nielsen Consumer Neuroscience study of 100 ads across 25 brands in the consumer goods market revealed that ads with the best emotional response generated a 23 percent lift in sales.[13] Emotional marketing is not merely effective as an engagement vehicle but also serves as a true business driver.

As Damasio says, "We are not thinking machines. We are feeling machines that think."

Grab Their Attention

There is value in getting in front of your audience and generating many brand touchpoints – even if you are not presenting a specific marketing message.

The "mere exposure effect" is a psychological phenomenon uncovered by the social psychologist Robert Zajonc in which people feel a preference for something due to familiarity. For example, if you see someone in the train on your morning commute to work every day, you start to trust them over time for no reason other than you are familiar with them.

Zajonc provides an example of the mere exposure effect in action in his article "Attitudinal Effects of Mere Exposure."[14] In an experiment conducted at Oregon State University, a person showed up to Speech 113 class wearing only a big black bag and sat at the back of the class. Only his bare feet were showing. At first, the other students looked at the unusual figure in disbelief and disgust. Their attitude was one of hostility.

However, as the weeks went by and the person in the bag kept attending class, the other students' attitude changed from hostility to curiosity, and then eventually changed to one of friendship. Without any additional knowledge, without knowing anything at all about him, they naturally started feeling like friends with this mysterious person.

Woody Allen once said that 80 percent of success in life was just showing up. As proven by the mere exposure effect, at a base level, your brand simply needs to show up, as well. You must find ways to get in front of your target audience repeatedly. By itself, just being present helps your brand break through initial resistance, and helps the brand to become a familiar entity in a potential customer's life.

This is why you see Coca-Cola advertisements all the time. It is not that Coke expects you to run out the door and buy a soda every time you see one of its ads. It is that the brand understands that the mere exposure effect can naturally lead to warm feelings towards the brand, so that the next time you are at the supermarket or by a vending machine, you will be more inclined to buy one.

When thinking about your marketing, though, remember that your audience is constantly being bombarded with marketing messages. Studies have shown that on average, your prospective customer encounters 3,000 to 5,000 marketing messages daily, not even counting social media. So, if you really want to embed your brand in prospects' minds, and get them to take notice and remember the brand, you will need to do more than just be visible.

What does it take to cut through the noise of thousands upon thousands of marketing messages every day?

Deviation!

When surprised, our attention immediately becomes focused. An anticipated pattern is disrupted in the mind, launching a neurobiological process that grabs our attention. The brain is naturally attracted to what is different.

The brain is actually hardwired to love surprises, as evidenced in neuroscientific studies led by Gregory S. Berns, M.D., Ph.D at Emory's Neuroimaging Group.[15] Using magnetic resonance imaging (MRI) to measure brain activity, Berns' team showed that the brain actively responds more to the unexpected than even to things a person likes or finds pleasurable.

The monthly razor subscription company Dollar Shave Club has utterly upended a mature industry with its series of jaw-dropping, laugh-out-loud videos, mocking the restrictions in drugstores that treat razor customers like felons or making fun of the excessive technology claims by the established players in the industry. Within 48 hours after launching its first video, nearly 12,000 people signed up for the subscription service. Within a few months, that exploded to 330,000. That first video? It now has more than 24 million views.

Deviating does not necessarily mean shock and awe, though. It just means being demonstrably different from the competition. Take the customer support software company Groove. Its blog first documented its rise from zero to $100K in monthly revenue and is now doing the same for its rise to $10 million annually. The blog reveals EVERYTHING, showing you every pimple and scratch along the way. Groove's level of transparency is unprecedented. It is such a departure from so much of today's marketing that puts a shiny sheen on every image, message, and brand touchpoint, that you cannot help but get sucked in and become a fan.

So, shake it up and be different. Really different! If your brand awareness and direct response activities at the top of the funnel are currently blending in with the massive amount of noise enveloping your audience, change course and craft your marketing for surprise and delight.

Not only does deviation help you to stand out among competing marketing messages, it also helps your target audience to remember you. Today's consumer or B2B buyer has a higher threshold for stimulation than in the past. If the messages they are consuming are similar, it becomes more difficult for the brain to do the work of figuring out which messages to remember. The more you can deviate from the other inputs, the more likely prospects are to recall your message when it is time to buy.

Cognitive Fluency

Once you get your target audience's attention, then what? Are you sure that you are effectively communicating with them?

In 1960, U.S. Navy aircraft engineer Kelly Johnson reportedly used the acronym KISS to remind everyone to "Keep It Simple, Stupid." The KISS principle is essentially the concept that systems work best when kept simple and therefore simplicity should be a goal in systems design.

It is the same in marketing. Take websites. It is not that people cannot comprehend complex tasks or navigate their way through inconsistent, byzantine navigation, but they will simply choose not to. Our brains are hard-wired to enjoy simplicity and ease-of-use and avoid complexity. A brand that delivers a simple, understandable experience will generate good feelings and will help website visitors feel an affinity towards it.

Think of it this way. If you instead offer up a website that puts the onus on your site visitor to figure out what you specifically offer, or why they should purchase from you, or even why they should give a hoot about you at all, then you are making it mentally harder for them to become a lead. What business in its right mind would voluntarily do this?

Our brains enjoy information processing when it is easy and intuitive. So, if you are looking to improve the marketing results from your website, you need to focus on improving your site visitors' ability to immediately and intuitively understand what is being presented and what the visitor should take away from the experience.

"Cognitive fluency" is the measure by which one's brain processes information. A high level of cognitive fluency means that something is easy for one's brain to process, whereas a low level means that something is relatively difficult to understand, to decipher, or to get through.

The key to understanding cognitive fluency is that it impacts not only your brain, but how you feel about something. In other words, the sensation of ease or difficulty in your thinking guides you to feel a certain way about it. If your site visitors become confused by what is on your web page, or if they have difficulty figuring out how to find what they are seeking on your site, guess what? A low level of cognitive fluency. Worse, it can result in a poor brand experience and negative feelings towards your brand as a whole. Whoa!

You can see the extensive effects of cognitive fluency throughout society and life. Psychologists have found that shares in companies with easier-to-pronounce names perform better than those with difficult-to-pronounce names. Even just changing the font of text on a page to something more legible can actually alter people's judgments about the veracity of the statement. Crazy, but true.

When your site visitors land on your website, their brains get to work. Physically, the retina converts what it is seeing on the page (the visual structure, images, headlines, messaging, calls-to-action, etc.) into electrical impulses, and these are transmitted to photoreceptor cells that deliver information to the brain, which then proceeds to code and store the information. This data can then be used by various parts of the brain for memory and perception. The more strenuous the effort to go through this process, the less enjoyable the experience. The easier the process, the more your site visitors associate good feelings with the experience. And all of this happens fast. Lightning fast.

In a 2012 Google Study, Google uncovered that your site visitors are judging your website's design within 50 milliseconds, and to a degree even within 17 milliseconds.[16] Talk about the need for cognitive fluency!

The study further found that visually complex websites are consistently rated as less beautiful than simpler sites. Complementary to this finding, the study revealed that site visitors tended to favor visually simple websites that fit an "industry mold." In other words, the more that a website generally adhered to a common category framework of website layout, the more that people reacted favorably to the site, as it was easier for their brains to process the information and convert that info into understanding.

Remember to keep it simple, and your marketing will be simply more effective.

Be Authentic

Even if you have the attention of your prospects and your messaging is easy to understand, you need to be wholly authentic if you hope to connect on a deeper level with your target audience. With so much clutter, noise, and marketing messaging enveloping us now, it has become easy for people to sniff out insincerity from brands that are courting them.

With the advent of social media and instant feedback, customers are now thinking more about openness and candor from the companies they patronize. For example, there are over one million Google searches annually for the words "authenticity" and "authentic". A 2016 Havas Worldwide study identified honesty/transparency as one of the three most important core values consumers feel brands should embody.[17] In Cohn & Wolfe's 2016 Authentic 100 study, the top brands were comprised of some of the most successful in the market, such as Disney, Amazon, Apple, VISA, Google, and Lego.[18] These are all brands that have demonstrated that they care about much more than just the bottom line.

According to the study, only 22 percent of Americans believe that brands are honest. With that said, though, the report highlights that consumers are yearning for authenticity, with nearly nine out of 10 consumers willing to take action to reward a brand for its authenticity by recommending it to others, pledging loyalty to the brand, etc.

We have been continually bombarded with so much marketing messaging that our minds now automatically tune out most of the noise. Being honest and showing your flaws in an open, vulnerable way is a path to cutting through the clutter, getting prospective customers to open their minds to your brand, and building a stronger relationship with your audience.

Domino's is an exemplary case of a company that did some soul searching, and then shared the results with customers in a remarkably authentic manner. As background, Domino's had always been known as a service oriented company and had long committed to delivering pizza in 30 minutes or less. However, over time, this obsession with speed created a perception among customers that there was no care put into the making of the food itself.

In the Domino's Pizza Turnaround, the company took customer feedback to heart, no matter how negative, and sought to revisit and remake its recipes from the dough up.

Actual focus group feedback at the time included, "Domino's pizza crust to me is like cardboard." "Worst excuse for pizza I've ever had." "The sauce tastes like ketchup." "Boring imitation of what pizza can be."

Most companies would get defensive and make excuses if faced with such criticism. Domino's, though, demonstrated its backbone and embraced the customer voices in order to turn its product around. Russell Weiner, former CMO and current President of Domino's in the U.S., explained to me that the only way to change things is to be 100 percent authentic and open. "You need to take it full on. You can't be only partly transparent." You need to be 100 percent honest and real. To that end, the company went so far as to hire a documentary filmmaker to do the initial Pizza Turnaround TV spot.

"We told the world, 'Our pizza sucks,'" Weiner said. "A great brand starts with a great product." And Weiner was fully determined to flip everything about the pizza on its head to achieve this.

With the harsh feedback in hand, Domino's top chefs got to work, exploring 10 types of crust, 15 sauces, and dozens of cheeses. They worked days, nights, and weekends until they hit upon new combinations that made them excited. For example, the crust was replaced with a rich, buttery version with garlic and herbs.

What caught my attention was Domino's unequivocal and relentless approach to the Pizza Turnaround. Weiner explained to me that all innovation reports into Marketing at Domino's, and this is a key to their success. When Domino's looks to innovate, it is not looking to offer a new product for a month as a promotion and then abandon it. Instead, it is looking for *real innovation*. The kind of innovation that hits the core of the business. The kind of innovation that is long-term. The kind of innovation where Domino's team will do anything to make the experience great. It does not even have to be about pizza.

And this is why Domino's dove in head first to the Pizza Turnaround in an effort to completely reinvent its pizza and win customers' hearts again.

An effective way to do this, Weiner continued, was to tell stories about the brand, using "double-click" marketing where the consumer digs deeper and deeper with each click to reach a more authentic picture of the brand. The Pizza Turnaround was a way for Domino's to share with customers the reinvention of its pizza from the inside-out. The company conducted a 360° campaign based on the tagline "Oh Yes We Did" to demonstrate the company's drive to do the unthinkable, sharing story after story of pizza gone wrong that was replaced with a better experience. Stories that made you understand without a doubt that Domino's was hellbent on radical improvement.

For example, one story that Weiner shared with me was a campaign to ensure that the delivery of pizza was just as good as the new, improved pizza itself. In this particular case, the cheese and toppings had slid off the top of the crust in transit to its residential destination. The consumer contacted Domino's, and the company rushed a video crew out to film the pizza, making the location of the Domino's franchise clear. What this did was cause an all-out dedication by franchisees across the country to take the commitment to quality to an entirely new extreme. Proactively broadcasting your own mistakes for the world to see, simply in the name of improving the customer experience? Oh Yes They Did!

The power of authenticity? From the Pizza Turnaround campaign, Domino's earned more than a billion impressions of free PR. Since the campaign, the company has been the fastest growing restaurant in the United States. Not just among pizza brands. Not just among fast food. The fastest growing restaurant, period.

Make It Visual

When you have your audience's attention, and you are communicating clearly in an authentic way, it's still important to understand how your audience processes input to the brain. This enables you to effectively get through and ensure your message is being remembered.

Your audience sees with their brains. In the book *Brain Rules*, author John Medina points out that roughly half of our brain's resources are dedicated to visual processing. The book explains the battle inside our brains between vision and our sense of smell. He points out that vision is winning the evolutionary fight: "More of our neurons are dedicated to vision than the other four senses combined, and olfactory cortex is losing ground to the visual cortex. About 60 percent of our smell-related genes have been permanently damaged in this neural arbitrage..."[19]

Need further proof of the power of vision? According to 3M, the human brain processes visuals 60,000 times faster than text.[20] Not six times faster. Not 600 times faster. Sixty-thousand times faster.

Let that sink in for a minute. If your audience can process visuals exponentially faster than text, it follows that you should evaluate your marketing to ensure you are communicating in a sufficiently visual way.

Yet, why is it that when you look at websites of many law firms, for example, it is as if the world has gone back to 1997? The sites have all the visual interest of a dictionary. The small images are overly "stock," stereotypical, and fake, and the messaging is boring. In my random review of 50 law firm websites, the average site dedicates more than 80 percent of the home page to text. My eyes quickly glazed over and it became a struggle to get through the list. Not exactly the most effective way to convince people to pick up the phone to call or complete an online form.

In *Brain Rules*, Medina tells the story of an experiment conducted at the epicenter of wine country.[21] French researchers at the University of Bordeaux brought together 54 of the best wine sommeliers in the world. These are folks with seemingly superhuman powers when it comes to wine tasting. In the world of wine, they use completely different vocabulary to describe a white wine from a red wine.

The researchers presented each of the 54 sommeliers with a glass of wine. It was in fact white wine, but the wine had been infused with odorless red dye before being brought out to the wine experts. In other words, the only difference was a visual one. The sommeliers were then asked to describe the wine.

How many of the world's best wine tasters do you think saw through the color ruse and accurately described the wine as white instead of its apparent red color? All of them? Ninety percent? Fifty percent?

Try zero! Not even one sommelier could mentally get past the visual color to recognize the wine's true nature. That is the power of vision. (Sorry, sense of smell, you lose.)

It is not only that vision trumps smell and other senses in its power to direct your brain and its corresponding translation of the world around you. Vision also leads to greater memory and recall. Your audience is better able to recognize and remember imagery over words. This is called the Pictorial Superiority Effect and helps explain why even though a person will remember 10 percent of the text they read three days later, when the words are paired with visuals, the recollection jumps to 65 percent.

In *Brain Rules*, there is a study involving 2,500 photos.[22] Test subjects, who were shown each picture, remembered them with approximately 90 percent accuracy several days after exposure. That is remarkable for such a large quantity of photos, but what is even more impressive is that each photo was shown for merely 10 seconds. Recall rates still hovered around 63 percent a year later.

As you prepare your next marketing campaign, ask yourself if the marketing is visual enough. As mentioned, the human brain processes visuals 60,000 times faster than text. It would be... well..., short-sighted if your marketing ignored this.

Mirror Neurons

Want to influence your target audience, guiding them to take action, to read your whitepaper, to register for your event, to download your free trial, or to make a purchase? Then it is time you start triggering mirror neurons in your marketing efforts.

What are mirror neurons? They are a set of cells that help you to experience what you see and hear. For example, your neurons fire in the same way when you smell chocolate or when you merely hear the word "chocolate."

Research involving monkeys in a lab in Parma, Italy highlights the power of mirror neurons. Scientists implanted electrodes in the brain of a monkey so that they could map the neurons that were controlling the monkey's movements.

Well, things went a bit haywire as one of the researchers, a grad student, entered the lab with an ice-cream cone. When the monkey watched him bring the cone to his mouth, there was a spike in the monkey's neural activity. In and of itself, that is not too astonishing or noteworthy. What makes the event truly remarkable is that the neurons that were set off were the very same ones used to move the monkey's own body. In other words, the monkey itself seemed to be having the experience of eating ice-cream merely by watching someone else do it.

For those of you old enough to understand the reference, think of seeing Marcia Brady of the Brady Bunch getting hit in the nose with a football (If you have no clue what I am talking about here, YouTube it![23]). You cannot help but cringe and feel her pain as the ball hits her face. It is just as if Peter Brady threw the ball at your own face. Eeeyouch!

Examining the inner working of our brains, here is what is

taking place behind the scenes. The premotor cortex is in the front area of the brain. This is the part of the brain where your body triggers its movements. The neurons fired from the premotor cortex provide instructions to the primary motor cortex, which sends out the signals that actually make you move.

It is theorized that these mirror neurons are also the way we empathize with others. We experience what others are experiencing through these mirror neurons, and that enables each of us to understand how others actually feel.

All told, these mirror neurons are crazy powerful. What this means for your marketing is that you should develop an experiential map for your brand, ideally through a journey or stories. The more you can paint a vivid picture, the better. Make it visceral. This is especially useful with case studies. Your site visitors will not only read or hear your story, they will live and experience it themselves through the power of mirror neurons.

Yet stories are not the only tool you can use. Visual input, such as videos, is another effective tool. The idea here is that you should "show" (not "tell") your audience what you want them to know. For example, do not just list a number of bland product benefits. Show them the benefits in action. Show them how they will feel when they use your products.

If during a brand touchpoint you want your audience to smell chocolate, or to achieve financial wealth through your services, or to get promoted due to gains from the implementation of your software, you now have the power to make them feel it. Weight Watchers does this with their "before and after" examples – its audience sees the "after" photos, and neurons are fired giving the feeling of weight loss achievement before any dieting or exercise even takes place.

Show your prospects the results they will experience using your product or service. Get them fired up. Make them feel the success. Mirror neurons are your friends.

People Fear Loss More Than They Seek Gain

In the documentary *The Armstrong Lie*, Lance Armstrong states, "I like to win, but more than anything, I can't stand this idea of losing. Because to me, losing means death."[24]

Well, we all know how that ended. Armstrong was so averse to losing he was willing to take steroids for years in order to artificially improve his cycling performance. The U.S. Anti-Doping Agency found that Armstrong had used performance-enhancing drugs and called him the ringleader of "the most sophisticated, professionalized and successful doping program that sport has ever seen." He received a lifetime ban and was stripped of all cycling accomplishments after 1998, including seven Tour de France titles.

Maybe he should have just focused on winning...

Armstrong clearly went in the wrong direction, but his obsession with loss aversion is revealing. Neuroscientific studies indicate that he was not alone. People fear loss more strongly than they seek gain. This aversion to loss is powerful and can be used effectively when showing prospective customers the negative effects caused by not purchasing your product or service.

What is especially surprising is that even if you present the same information to the prospect but frame it in the sense of loss rather than gain, your conversions can increase. For example, instead of speaking to how your product saves the prospect money, tell them how making the purchase will help them avoid losing money.

The concept of "loss aversion" was first demonstrated by the psychologists Amos Tversky and Daniel Kahneman.[25] Tversky was a Professor of Behavioral Sciences at Stanford University. He earned widespread attention in 1988 when he released a study during the NBA basketball playoffs showing that a basketball player is no more likely to make his or her next shot after successfully making one. Kahneman is a professor at Princeton University. He won the Nobel Memorial Prize in Economic Sciences, and his book *Thinking, Fast and Slow* is a New York Times bestseller.

Kahneman argues that people are poor at making decisions about what will make them happy. Quantifying people's predilection for loss aversion, Kahneman found that most people are approximately twice as sensitive to potential losses as to potential gains.

A UCLA study was the first to provide neural evidence that people are hard-wired to avoid loss more than seek gain.[26] The study examined the behavior of people who were given 250+ opportunities to gamble with $30, with a 50-50 chance of winning each time. For example, would they agree to a coin toss in which you could win $30 but could just as easily lose $20? On average, with the risk of losing $10, participants in the study needed the chance to win $19 in order to accept the gamble. That is a figure well beyond what the typical investor would consider a highly profitable return over the course of two or even three years. The study found that the reward center of the brain responds not only to actual gain and loss, but to *potential* gain and loss.

In everyday terms, loss aversion is the reason why you might stay in your seat for an entire movie, even though a few minutes into the movie you have already realized that it is a stinker. You have already paid for the ticket and so in your mind there is more pain associated with wasting the money than sitting for another two hours through a movie that you just do not enjoy.

The automated investment service Betterment provides a marketing example of the power of loss aversion. Betterment uses messages like "Stop losing money to fees" to make site visitors anxious about losing money to excessive fees. They then take that message further by detailing the different types of fees site visitors should worry about losing, such as trade fees, transaction fees, and rebalancing fees.

In your own marketing, it is worth rethinking whether you are exclusively focused on the gains that your audience would derive by purchasing from you or whether it would enhance your results to also highlight the pain they will feel by not buying from you.

Get Them To Remember You

As humans, perceptions of a brand are formed through associations developed in the mind. As mentioned, the human brain contains approximately 100 billion neurons, and these neurons interact to the tune of trillions of synapses, or connections that pass electrical or chemical signals between the neurons.

For example, when I think of the brand Seventh Generation, makers of plant-based products for the home, I think of green. I think of environmentalism. I think of the leaf logo. I think of a B Corporation. I think of political activism. I even think of the Lorax and Ellen. Yes, Ellen DeGeneres.

Why is it that the Lorax and Ellen would come to mind? In line with the brand's green ethos, it partnered with The Lorax upon the movie's release, with the fluffy, orange guardian of the forest appearing in Seventh Generation's ads and packaging. On Earth Day, the brand sponsored the popular TV show "Ellen".

In order to understand and interpret the world around us, our brains form associations. This makes it easier for us to remember all the various pieces of our lives and make decisions accordingly. Humans actually have the largest association cortex, which enables us to form complex mental functions beyond basic sensory stimulation.

You may believe that when your audience encounters your brand's marketing, there is a linear progression of thoughts in their minds as they intake the messaging, content, and visuals. The reality is messier than this. One idea may trigger an avalanche of other ideas concurrently.

The human brain stores and retrieves information through neural networks of association. The involvement of multiple senses helps to create stronger memories. It is not necessarily that one phrase or image in your marketing is creating a meaningful imprint on your audience's brains, but rather that it is triggering a vast array of associations.

This is why it is powerful for you to appeal to various senses in your marketing. I talked about the value of visual marketing earlier in this chapter. Beyond that, the more associations you create, the more likely that the associations cut indelible grooves in the connections inside your audience's minds. Make them feel something. Deliver an experience.

A brand's impact can be powerful when a brand has built an ecosystem of mental associations. It is almost impossible for me, for example, to *not* think of the green leaf logo, political activism, and the Lorax when I think of Seventh Generation.

When delivering a brand experience filled with associations, do it over and over and over again. Repeated firing of the same nerve cells helps to rewire the brain with positive associations.

It is surprising how many businesses and brands treat each marketing campaign in a silo, yet have never spent the time or energy building the brand to help forge strong associations in the minds of their audience.

How about your brand? Can you define an ecosystem of brand associations? What is your Lorax?

Rethink How They Think

This chapter provides new insights into how your customers and prospective customers think. As you can see, there is much more going on inside their thinking than what is apparent on a surface level. As a marketer, it is helpful to your efforts to understand as much about them as possible. After all, they are people, just like you.

Even though every individual is unique, everyone is human and the human brain has certain characteristics that are universal. By gaining a deeper understanding of the brain, neuroscience, human psychology, and behavior, you can align your marketing to what will move your audience most effectively.

Some fans of Harley-Davidson tattoo the Harley logo on their bodies. I am not suggesting that is a yardstick by which to measure your ability to bond with your audience, but it is remarkable and provides you with an appreciation for just how powerful branding can be. There is clearly more to your marketing than just impressions, clicks, and a product description. The market is too cluttered for that. If you are stuck or simply looking to drive greater growth, try rethinking how your prospects think. Strive to connect with them on a much deeper level, one aligned to their subconscious, and then watch the magic start to happen.

Chapter Summary

Brain science offers you a way to transform your marketing into something more powerful and more effective. If your marketing today somewhat resembles an encyclopedia, where you are focused on plainly explaining your products and services in as much detail as possible, be prepared to start over.

Devise methods to communicate and engage with your prospective customers on a subconscious level. Make sure you are being authentic in everything you do, that you are evoking an emotional response, and that you are helping your audience to build brand associations in their minds.

Dig deeper and learn as much as you can about the way your audience thinks. The more you understand how they think, the greater the insights you will glean into why they do what they do, why they behave the way they behave, and why they buy what they buy.

- Review your marketing. Is it focused exclusively on the rational, conscious level?
- Is your marketing essentially stating what it is you sell, rather than focusing on the reasons your audience should feel compelled to purchase from you?
- What are ways for you to communicate with your audience on a more subconscious level?
- How can your marketing evoke an emotional response from your prospective customers?
- Are you inadvertently forcing prospects to work hard at

understanding what you offer, why they should care, and why you are a better option than the competition? How can you simplify your messaging for more direct and immediate understanding?

- Is your marketing visual enough, or are you overly reliant on text?
- Your audience is constantly being bombarded with marketing messaging. How can you cut through the noise by deviating from the rest of the pack and surprising them?
- How can you activate the mirror neurons in your audience's brains to point to an aspirational version of themselves?
- What mental associations can you build for your brand in their minds?

3

RETHINK YOUR GOALS

A study by BetterWorks, a developer of strategic planning software, found that organizations that use formal goal setting exercises are 3.5X more likely to be in the top tier of financial performers every year. The same research found that only seven percent of employees understand their company's business strategies and what is expected of them to help achieve company goals.[1]

Yikes!

Most marketing teams establish marketing goals to drive growth. However, when the goals are vague, undocumented, and lack a tracking and accountability infrastructure, they often go unrealized. This is because these attributes are all silent killers of marketing goals, and therefore ultimately of business growth.

Through several decades of working with a wide variety of companies across multiple industries, I have often found that marketing teams sabotage their own success by failing to conduct goal setting in a way that provides powerful direction, fuels momentum, and ensures alignment of all marketing activities.

When the result is being 3.5X more likely to be a top performer, why would your marketing team be anything but totally fanatical about goal setting, goal management, and goal achievement? Before onboarding any new client at Stratabeat, our marketing agency, we always ask for the company's marketing goals. It is where we always start, as we know that with the right goals, your marketing can follow a direct path to growth.

The Beauty Of An Airplane

Want to travel towards your marketing goals at 550 miles per hour?

Think of an airplane. The sky eliminates barriers and clears the way for your flight to sail through the sky at speeds of 500 to 600 mph in a direct line with your destination. Your navigational system ensures you are going in the right direction, and even if you need to make adjustments during the trip, the system recalculates exactly where to go next so that you are always in an optimal position to reach your destination in the fastest time possible.

Might you hit turbulence during your journey? Sure. Your momentum, though, is not thrown off course by it. Rather, it is something to work your way through, while still completely focused on reaching the destination.

Now, compare that with the way that some marketing teams operate. I see it as the journey of a car in a crowded city as compared to an airplane in flight. Distractions, traffic, stop signs, roundabouts, U-turns, "Do Not Enter" signs, and potholes. Not exactly the easiest way to get to where you want to go.

Your organization may establish annual goals. You may even be creating quarterly goals. Where you might be tripping up, though, is with everything that happens from that point onwards in utilizing the goals towards a clear, focused outcome within a specific time period. Is your goal achievement infrastructure configured like an airplane flying through the sky, or does it resemble a car making its way through crowded city streets? Is your infrastructure teeing you up for marketing success? Or is it ill-defined and failing in delivering a crystal clear daily direction to propel your progress?

If you want to inject new growth in your business, revamp your goal achievement methodology – your approach, tools, and processes. You will still need to execute your marketing effectively in order to achieve massive results, but the proper goals infrastructure enables you to extract the compounded energy of an entire team that is going in a clear direction for clear purposes every day of the year.

Proving What Works

Gail Matthews, Professor of Psychology at Dominican University, conducted a goal setting study to uncover factors that lead to a higher rate of goal achievement.[2] A total of 149 marketers, entrepreneurs, attorneys, bankers, vice presidents, directors of non-profits, and others from around the world participated. They were separated into five groups defined by conditions:

- Group 1 was asked to think about their goals
- Group 2-5 were asked to write down their goals
- Group 3 was also asked to form action commitments
- Group 4 was asked to form action commitments and

send their goals and commitments to a supportive friend
- Group 5 did the same as Group 4 but were also sent weekly reminders and asked to email quick progress reports to their friend

After four weeks, participants were asked to rate their progress toward achieving their goals. Average goals attained were:

- Group 1 – 4.28
- Group 2 – 6.08
- Group 3 – 5.08
- Group 4 – 6.41
- Group 5 – 7.60

Group 5 achieved significantly more than all the other groups. Group 4 achieved more than Groups 1, 2, and 3. Group 2 achieved significantly more than Group 1.

The difference between non-written goal Group 1 and the other four groups was significant. Group 5 outperformed Group 1 by 78 percent. The mean average of the non-written group was 4.28 goals achieved while the average for the other four groups combined was 6.44 – 50 percent higher achievement rate for the written goals groups. Any way you look at it, documenting goals led to significantly improved goal achievement in the study.

That is the power of effective goal setting. If you are going to rejuvenate your marketing results, starting with clear, specific, documented goals is essential. Without them, you will waste time, energy, and resources. Documented goals act as a filter for your team's marketing activities, and similarly act as a filter for what *not* to spend time on. New opportunities continually arise and can easily become the very distractions that prevent achievement of your goals. Documenting specific goals is an effective way to keep your entire team on track towards measurable progress in a highly focused, efficient, and productive style.

Difficult Goals Produce The Highest Levels Of Performance

Experimental psychologist Thomas Ryan was an early advocate of goal setting theory and in 1970 advanced the premise that goals affect action. Professor Edwin A. Locke at the Robert H. Smith School of Business at the University of Maryland and Gary P. Latham at the University of Toronto's Rotman School of Management built on Ryan's work and found a positive, linear relationship that the most difficult goals produced the highest levels of effort and performance.

In *Building a Practically Useful Theory of Goal Setting and Task Motivation – A 35-Year Odyssey,* Locke and Latham summarize 35 years of research into goal setting.[3] Locke and Latham identify the following ways that goals affect performance.

First, goals provide direction. They direct attention and effort toward goal-relevant activities and away from distractions – both in thought and action. The more that your team's various activities are aligned towards your specific marketing goals, the easier it becomes to achieve them.

Second, goals fuel energy. The higher the goal, the greater the effort expended to reach it. Set your goals low and your team will likely underachieve its potential. Set them aggressively, and your team will actually achieve much more.

Third, goals drive persistence. When faced with a difficult goal, participants work towards it longer. Persistence is an underappreciated attribute in helping teams break through obstacles and overcome hiccups. If you want your team achieving its marketing goals, persistence is critical.

Setting clear, specific goals provides direction, fuels your energy, and drives your persistence. Think of a car trip. Getting into a car without a motor or gas or a specific destination is just silly. But that is what you would be doing if you set up a marketing program without documented goals.

Why Are So Many Companies Unclear About Their Goals?

As the BetterWorks study pointed out, only seven percent of employees reported that they fully understand what is expected of them to help achieve company goals.

Let's be honest. That's just ridiculous. Why is it that so many companies have vague goals, or undocumented goals, or are constantly changing their goals?

In running our agency, Stratabeat, we talk with many companies on a regular basis. During our first meeting, we always ask about marketing goals. Sometimes, the client is extremely clear and can rattle off the goals without hesitation. Yet other times, we are met with vagueness, such as "to increase revenue" or "to grow leads" or "to take things to another level." All of these can be interpreted in countless ways. Meaning, the client has no real goals.

While just about every company wants to grow, only some have thought through the details about what is required to attain profitable growth. They sometimes mention revenue growth without thinking about how that correlates to profits or profit margins or costs. Or growth in revenue from existing customers vs. new customers. Or growth by geography.

At many companies, if you ask 10 people about their organizational goals, you will get 10 different answers. Why is that? It is clear they do not understand the power of effective goal setting as a growth driver.

Let me be clear. Vagueness kills growth. If you want to spur significant growth at your company, get ready to become obsessed with goal setting, goal tracking, and goal achievement.

Speaking of being obsessed with goal management, allow me to introduce you to Provenir, a provider of risk analytics software. When Adi Bachar-Reske joined the company as Global Head of Marketing, there were no goal setting mechanisms or metrics in place. She knew this would be an obstacle to growth and so quickly remedied that situation by transforming the culture into one obsessed with goals, metrics, and measurement.

Bachar-Reske immediately established a twice-annual goal setting strategy at an extremely detailed level. She outlined goals for the company website, content creation, announcements, and webinars. She established specific targets for leads, social media followers, registration for events, and conversions.

But she did not stop there. She then developed a comprehensive plan to meet these ambitious goals, setting up a master calendar and a detailed campaign program complete with spend, social interactions, and lead opportunities.

Finally, she clearly communicated to the team what had been accomplished in the way of lead generation and sales conversion.

There is no misunderstanding or lack of clarity when it comes to goals and expectations at Provenir. That is the type of detailed planning that will lead to revenue growth and business success. That is using goal setting to rethink a marketing operation.

iMotions, developer of a biometric research platform that enables execution of multi-sensor human behavior research projects (mentioned in the *Rethink Your Audience* chapter), is also committed to clear goal setting.

"We have three main goals we drive towards," said CEO Peter Hartzbech. "First a clear goal of amount of inbound marketing qualified leads we drive. Those lead generation goals are set based on lead to opportunity win conversion rates and calculated based on our sales goals and are broken down into quarterly and monthly goals. Second, we set a goal on the number of subscribers to our newsletter and third, we have a goal based on brand value based on brand searches. Establishing those goals keeps the marketing team focused on what really matters, and how the different activities map to those goals."

WP Engine, a website hosting platform for WordPress sites with the largest group of WordPress developers in the world (mentioned in the *Rethink Your Audience* chapter), has a set of specific goals that are measured at a minimum bi-annually and many that are reviewed monthly or weekly.

"My philosophy is that the brand must equal business, so teams are required to link the business case to any effort we undertake," explained CMO Mary Ellen Dugan. "A few key brand metrics we track include: Unaided Awareness and Brand of Choice. These are tracked on a bi-annual basis and done through an external study. On a monthly/quarterly basis we track our social and content engagement metrics to see trends in general interest.

"From a demand generation perspective, we track Prospects, MQLs (marketing qualified leads) and opportunities, as well as all conversion metrics on paid media," Dugan continued.

"Finally, as a technology company, we are very interested in tracking our own site metrics and performance."

Such a detailed goals achievement framework has helped WP Engine to, as mentioned previously, increase its business from roughly 40,000 customers to more than 60,000 in the past year. Goal setting works!

Vision-Based Framework For Goal-Setting

According to Rand Fishkin, founder and former CEO of Moz and Co-Founder of Inbound.org, companies that have gone from startup to scale to world-changing status have a common architecture that is vision-based and mission-driven. Goal setting then flows from the core purpose and core values.

"Our marketing goals are aligned fairly precisely to the business's most important yearly and quarterly initiatives," Fishkin told me. He shared a flowchart to illustrate the vision-based framework[4] that Moz operates within and that is used to propel the future direction of the company. Moz refers to it as the "architecture behind our decisions, infusing all of our efforts."

The process begins by defining the core purpose of the company – why it exists – and then defining the organization's core values. Core values are the essential and enduring tenets of the organization – a small set of timeless guiding principles.

The next step is establishing a strategic vision that takes what you want to achieve and develops a plan to get there. From there, Moz develops its BHAGs (Big Hairy Audacious Goals), which Fishkin believes are critical to counterbalance the fixed core ideology with a relentless drive for progress.

Fishkin provided the example of Sam Walton, who in 1945 set

the BHAG to "make my little Newport store the best, most profitable in Arkansas within five years." He continued to add BHAGs including the goal of becoming a $125 billion company by the year 2000. In 2016, Walmart's total revenue was more than $482 billion.

All of Moz's goals and strategic initiatives flow out of this vision-based process.

"That said, we also make sure to maintain time and bandwidth for creative projects that aren't intended to have direct ROI, but are focused on helping our community and the broader world of SEO," Fishkin added. "That's a big part of who we are, and what built the company in the first place. Our mission isn't just about software or signups or profits, but about making web marketing a more transparent, accessible practice."

In Fishkin's presentation *Growing Moz: 8 Lessons Learned - #7 Our Greatest Wins Have All Come from Serendipity*, Fishkin points out that despite being a very analytics-focused company, many of its greatest wins have come from serendipity – happy accidents.[5] He uses the example of meeting someone at a conference outside your industry that through a series of events leads to meeting another person who ends up leading a round of investment for the company.

One of the rules on the Moz marketing team is to allocate 20 percent of the budget to non-measurable, serendipitous forms of marketing. In other words, it is important to have clear goals, but you should also allow for a bit of experimentation in a self-contained way that not only mitigates risk but also opens the door to game-changing serendipity.

The goal achievement architecture at Moz has helped guide the company to 274 percent growth over the past five years.[6]

Goal Science Thinking

One of the latest developments in goal setting theory is the introduction of goal science thinking. The concept builds on the traditional Objectives and Key Results (OKR) system of goal setting pioneered by Intel's Andy Grove and Oracle's Gary Kennedy in the mid-1980's.

BetterWorks is using Goal Science Thinking as the basis for helping companies achieve success. With Goal Science Thinking, goals can have multiple contributors across various teams and departments – a significant departure from OKR. "We always see better performance on goals with cross-functional contributors," says BetterWorks CEO Kris Duggan.

Consistency is also key to Goal Science Thinking. "For anyone who makes a point of setting goals, there's always the danger of setting and forgetting – in fact most people do," states Duggan. "You have to be incredibly regular in viewing them, assessing them, and measuring progress against them to stand any chance."[7]

Goals = Action

Regardless of methodology or process, goal setting has a long-proven record of leading to action. In 1961, President John F. Kennedy set a goal of putting a man on the moon by the end of the decade. Seven years later Neil Armstrong took "one small step for man and one giant leap for mankind." The goal reignited America's "can-do" spirit and resulted in a decade of technological advancement.

Identifying goals is one of the most powerful – and important –

things a company can do. **Goals compel action. Goals** *become* **action.**

When Microsoft was merely a 30-person team based in Albuquerque, it was driven by a singularly bold and ambitious goal.

"Early on, Paul Allen and I set the goal of a computer on every desk and in every home," related Bill Gates in an email he sent to employees in 2015 celebrating the 40th anniversary of the company. "It was a bold idea and a lot of people thought we were out of our minds to imagine it was possible. It is amazing to think about how far computing has come since then, and we can all be proud of the role Microsoft played in that revolution."[8]

Industry giants such as Digital Equipment Corporation's (DEC) co-founder Ken Olsen scoffed at the idea saying, "There is no reason for any individual to have a computer in his home."[9] Microsoft came to dominate the desktop operating system (OS) and applications markets and is now an $85 billion+ company.[10] DEC? It fell into a downward spiral that ultimately led to its acquisition by Compaq and subsequently Hewlett Packard two decades later.

But even Microsoft did not have all the answers.

In 2007, Steve Jobs announced Apple's goal of "reinventing the phone" with the release of the iPhone. Steve Ballmer, head of Microsoft at the time responded, "There's no chance that the iPhone is going to get any significant market share. No chance."[11]

By 2013, the iPhone had captured over 40 percent of the U.S. smartphone market.[12]

Never underestimate the power of goals to drive action and fuel ambitious achievement.

Stick To Your Goals Like Glue

Even if your company's goals are not as ambitious as those of JFK, Microsoft, or Apple, they still must be crystal clear and well defined. Many companies end up being vague with their goals, confusing their staff. In his book *Mighty Midsized Companies: How Leaders Overcome 7 Silent Growth Killers*, Robert Sher points to endless "tinkering at the top" of an organization as one of the most common reasons for midsized companies failing.[13] You must STICK TO YOUR GOALS, even in the face of adversity. It is simply too easy to keep changing one's mind, endlessly chasing after "the next big thing" or "flavor of the day."

Sher illustrates the point with the example of cell phone accessories company Cellairis. Taki Skouras, twin brother Joseph, and Jamie Brown started Cellairis in Atlanta in 2000 to take advantage of the cell phone boom. Their idea was to leverage cheap retail space – carts in the middle of shopping malls – to sell cell phone cases primarily, along with other accessories. In five years, they had built a $50 million business.

In 2006, the tinkering began. According to Sher, instead of sticking with their original goal of selling accessories, on the advice of the new company president they expanded into selling phone service. They partnered with AMP'd Mobile and began selling the service without testing the strategy.

AMP'd wasn't charging enough for the service and extended credit to bad risk customers and not surprisingly, filed for bankruptcy nine months later. Cellairis and the wireless providers whose services AMP'd were reselling were left holding the bag and never got paid.

Distracted by the joint venture, Cellairis' revenue dropped by a third in one year. Getting out from under the AMP'd partnership cost them millions of dollars. Tinkering had cost them dearly. Fortunately for the company, the founders quickly recognized their error and refocused on their original core business. Closing out Sher's story, he reports that revenue bounced back and reached $350 million in 2013.

Sher points out that CFOs play a valuable role in keeping C-suite leaders from tinkering. "The most successful CFO's I know insist their company's core strategy be written down," Sher says in an article he wrote for the Harvard Business Review. "Such discipline creates focus."[14]

Not only is it important to stick to goals once they are established, it is important to be consistent in the pursuit of such goals. I can say that, based on having worked with more than 100 different companies through the years on their marketing efforts, waffling on goals at the top is a surefire way to derail a brand's marketing efforts. On-again off-again efforts force an organization to expend a great deal more energy than consistent, focused efforts.

Planes use the most fuel during takeoff, not when cruising at high altitude. Inconsistency in focus on corporate goals means that your organization will spend excessive time on taking off over and over again, instead of making massive progress while in cruise control. If you keep changing your goals over and over again, you will fail when faced with a competitor that is focused and persistently going all out towards its established goals.

The compound effect is one of the key reasons consistency pays off when it comes to goals achievement. Darren Hardy, former publisher of SUCCESS magazine and author of the New York Times bestseller, *The Compound Effect*, demonstrates the power of consistency in the book. He gives you a choice: take $3 million in cash right now on the spot, or take a penny today and then double it every day for a month.

Choosing the $3 million provides an immediate windfall – and instant gratification. Making that choice, however, leaves millions of dollars on the table. Taking a penny and doubling it will generate only two cents after two days and 16 cents after five days. Not too encouraging. Even after 29 days, the $3 million choice looks smarter, but that all changes on the 30th day when the total amount would be more than $5.3 million. And on the 31st day it would exceed $10.7 million.[15]

We are taught from an early age with the story of the Tortoise and the Hare that slow and steady wins the race. When it comes to your corporate goals, consistency to achieve success is more than a fable. Starting out takes a great deal of effort, but once you get rolling you will often experience the hockey stick effect and results come much more easily.

Remember the words of Steve Jobs, "I'm convinced that about half of what separates the successful entrepreneurs from the non-successful one is pure perseverance."

Narrow Your Focus

What defines truly great leaders is not necessarily what they do but what they do *not* do. When Steve Jobs returned to Apple in 1997, the company had not reported a profit in over a year. He reduced a completely bloated product line back to four products, and in January of 1998 he announced Apple earned a $45 million profit in the last quarter of 1997.

Jobs outlined Apple's intense focus during an interview with Fortune: "Apple is a $30 billion company, yet we've got less than 30 major products. I don't know if that's ever been done before.

Certainly, the great consumer electronics companies of the past had thousands of products. We tend to focus much more," Jobs said. "People think focus means saying yes to the thing you've got to focus on. But that's not what it means at all. It means saying no to the hundred other good ideas that there are. You have to pick carefully.

"I'm actually as proud of many of the things we haven't done as the things we have done," Jobs went on. "The clearest example was when we were pressured for years to do a PDA, and I realized one day that 90 percent of the people who use a PDA only take information out of it on the road. They don't put information into it."[16]

When Mark Parker took the CEO position at Nike, he talked with Steve Jobs. He asked Jobs if he had any advice for him, and initially Jobs said no. But then said that he actually did have one suggestion for Parker.

"Well, just one thing," said Jobs. "Nike makes some of the best products in the world. Products that you lust after. But you also make a lot of crap. Just get rid of the crappy stuff and focus on the good stuff."

Parker thought that after a brief silence Jobs would laugh and tell Parker that he was joking. There was indeed a silence. Jobs, however, did not laugh. He was dead serious about narrowing one's focus.[17]

In the book *The 4 Disciplines of Execution: Achieving Your Wildly Important Goals*, authors Sean Covey, Chris McChesney, and Jim Huling write about the importance of narrowing your focus. "Basically the more you try to do, the less you actually accomplish," they write. "This is a stark, inescapable principle that we all live with.

"The sun's scattered rays are too weak to start a fire, but once you focus them with a magnifying glass, they will bring paper to flame in seconds," the authors go on. "The same is true of human beings – once their collective energy is focused on a challenge, there is little they can't accomplish."[18]

Warren Buffett says you have to "marry your priorities" to achieve success. He says you must first list your top 25 priorities. Then, circle your top five. As a result, you have two lists – your top five priorities and the next 20. Buffett implores you to delete these 20. It is these 20 that are the real threat to your ability to achieve results, as they represent the many distractions that will prevent you from achieving your most important goals. They are your "avoid at all cost list." He stresses that without priorities, nothing gets done and that focus is the only way to avoid distractions that can derail your success.[19]

Narrowing your focus is key when setting goals.

Jim Collins, author of *Good to Great* says, "If you have more than three priorities, you have no priorities."[20]

The benefits of setting fewer goals are easy to see. By focusing all of your company's assets, resources, and brainpower on three things, you are more likely to achieve amazing results. Splinter your attention among many goals, and you dilute your resources and minimize the attention you can pay to each of them.

Having many goals also reduces the importance of all of them. The feeling may be that just achieving some of them is acceptable, which leads to a certain level of complacency and rationalization that since you achieved some of your goals, you actually did pretty well.

Narrow your focus, and you will exponentially increase the likelihood of achieving your goals.

"SMART" Goals

If your marketing team has not written down its goals, where do you start? Many executives today subscribe to the method called SMART goals. The acronym guides you as you develop effective goals that help you achieve success. The initials stand for:

- Specific
- Measurable
- Achievable
- Relevant
- Time-Bound

The idea of SMART criteria is commonly attributed to Peter Drucker in the fifties as part of his Management by Objectives (MBO) philosophy of defining specific objectives and conveying them to members of the organization and working to achieve each one. George T. Doran, a consultant and former Director of Corporate Planning for Washington Water Power Company, first used it as a term in an article he published in 1981.

The idea of SMART goals is that your marketing team will behave much differently if your goal is to "increase U.S. sales of your newest product line by $5 million in the next 12 months" vs. a generic goal of "increasing sales." To be effective, goals should follow the SMART formula.

Be Specific

To develop clear goals, you must start by being specific. Very specific. Goals must be detailed enough not only to identify particular opportunities but to have enough detail to allow you to measure progress toward their achievement.

"Increasing sales" is not specific enough. You need to specify exactly what growth you want to achieve and in what market or product line. "Double online sales of Product A while increasing in-store sales of Product B by 15 percent in the next year" is a specific goal.

Use the same format if you are talking about your marketing campaigns. Be specific about your target conversion volume, cost-per-conversion, and conversion rate, for example.

Without specificity, what is acceptable becomes vague and elastic. It is only with highly specific goals that expectations and actions can be fully aligned.

Be Measurable

"What gets measured, gets done," has been a familiar management mantra for many years. Measure everything! In this day and age, there is absolutely no excuse for a lack of measurement, no matter what your team's goals may be.

Measuring accomplishes several things. First, it sets targets that often spark the competitive juices in people and spurs them to action. Second, it establishes accountability for groups or individuals and lets the world know what is expected. Finally, it allows you to track progress and alter behavior to help achieve the goal.

That final point is a crucial one and is perfectly illustrated when comparing old time boxing to basketball. In the old days of smoke-filled boxing rings, the fighters would come out for 12 or 15 three-minute rounds, slug it out and then head back to their corners. Three judges would score the round on their own cards but no one – not the fans, nor the fighters – would know what those scores were. Unless one fighter knocked out the other, no one would know who won until the end of the fight when the judge's cards would be announced and the referee would raise the hand of the winner.

There were many times the fans and fighters did not agree with the decision but the result was final. If the losing fighter knew he was behind, he may have altered his behavior to affect the outcome but he had no idea of how he was doing.

Contrast that with a basketball game where a giant scoreboard hangs over the center of the arena for all to see. There is no question about who is winning or losing since every basket is meticulously documented as soon as it occurs. If one team is down by ten points with five minutes to play, the coach and team members know they have to change tactics in order to get back in the game. If they fall short, they know it immediately – there are no last-minute surprises.

Jeffrey Hayzlett, former CMO at Kodak, Chairman of C-Suite Holdings, and bestselling author of *The Mirror Test, Running the Gauntlet,* and *Think Big, Act Bigger: The Rewards of Being Relentless*, and introduced to you in the *Rethink How They Think* chapter, shared his opinion on the importance of measurement with me, "Why would you have a goal if you can't measure it? It seems kind of ridiculous, in my opinion, because everything should be measurable – especially your goals – in one way or another.

"Typically most marketers' success is going to be judged by their ability to increase sales, increase margins for the business or products, increase customer satisfaction and increase brand awareness," Hayzlett goes on. "There are various tactics or sub-objectives you could put around those but by-and-large those are the things you are going to be measured upon. When I look at my own brand, or one of the companies I own or work with, I use those same guidelines."

Measuring sales revenue and the number of new clients landed is easy. Measuring clicks and conversions is easy. Measuring registrations and subscriptions is easy. You can now even measure such warm and fuzzy elements as sentiment and loyalty. To not measure is to not have clear goals.

You want to be playing basketball, not be boxing in the dark.

Be Achievable

When establishing your goals, you need to strike a balance between goals that are too easy and ones that are too difficult. Set the bar too low and you jeopardize the feeling of accomplishment. On the other hand, setting a goal that is clearly not reachable will only serve to demotivate and reduces the chances of success.

The attainability of a goal is often the result of the resources made available to the team. Dedicating a chunk of the budget or more of the team's time to the goal sends a very clear signal to everyone involved. If when JFK set the goal of reaching the moon he also had cut NASA's budget, chances are Armstrong would never have taken his stroll on the lunar surface. If you are unable to provide adequate resources for a particular goal, you will have to adjust the goal accordingly.

One major problem with goals that are simply unattainable is that they make failure excusable. Everyone on the team can too easily laugh off and dismiss the goal as having never been of a serious nature. The entire exercise becomes an inside joke.

Be sure you are pushing your team hard, but that the goals you put into place are achievable. (More on this later in this chapter...)

Be Relevant

For goals to drive desired behavior, they should relate to the overall strategic direction of your company and to the people in it. They must be worth the cost and resources you plan to devote to attaining them, and it must be the right time to be taking on the particular goals you have set.

Establishing relevancy means making sure your marketing goals align with your company's mission, beliefs, and values, while also ensuring your team has the necessary knowledge, skills, and tools for attainment. Your team should not only be aware of the goals, but should also feel strongly about them.

The bottom line: your goals have to matter.

Be Time-Bound

It is essential that your goals have a specified timeframe. If Kennedy's goal in 1962 was to "someday put a man on the moon," it would have lost all its power. Setting the deadline of a lunar landing "by the end of the decade" infused the goal with the sense of urgency and motivation that eventually enabled it to be achieved.

A deadline ensures focused efforts and prevents distractions from other routine tasks that will come up. The restricted time becomes the impetus that drives motivation and keeps the goal on track.

Use deadlines to increase your team's productivity. People tend to take as much time as they are given on a specific task. By shortening the deadline, you heighten the sense of urgency and increase output. Here is where great teams become exceptional. Steve Jobs was notorious for setting aggressive deadlines in driving his teams to achieve more and more.

Regardless of how you break it down, you should always ensure that your goals have a defined time element.

Marrying SMART Goals With Stretch Goals

SMART goals are an essential first step, but you cannot stop there. As New York Times reporter Charles Duhigg points out in his book *Smarter Faster Better: The Secrets of Being Productive in Life and Business*, you will achieve more if you couple your SMART goals with stretch goals.[21] Duhigg believes you can be much more effective if you balance larger goals with smaller goals.

In his book, Duhigg discusses the dangers of "cognitive closure," our desire to solve a problem quickly rather than taking our time and allowing solutions to come to us. This is why stretch goals need to be part of the equation. Although cognitive closure feels productive, there is a significant difference between being busy and actually getting important things done. Stretch goals help you to get out of the "downward spiral of busyness," and to continually push your efforts towards more ambitious, important achievements.

Start at the end with larger, longer-term goals. Work backwards to smaller and smaller "enabling" goals. As you tackle your smaller SMART goals, you will have your stretch goals in mind, forcing a calibration towards what is important rather than what is easy to complete.

In his book, Duhigg points to the experience of GE's airplane engine division as an example of the success of this process. GE had begun system goal setting as early as the 1940's, but by the 1980's results from some of its larger divisions were falling.

During a visit to Japan in 1993, CEO Jack Welch learned about the development of the country's high-speed "bullet trains" that travelled at an average speed of 120 mph. Engineers had first estimated that the top "realistic" speed would be 75 mph. When the head of the railway system insisted that was not good enough, the engineers deployed hundreds of innovations to eventually "break through" and reach the higher speed goal.

Welch believed he could adapt the "bullet train" thinking to his operation and proposed marrying GE's established SMART goals with what he termed "stretch goals" and "using dreams to set business targets – with no real idea of how to get there. If you *do* know how to get there – it's not a stretch target," he insisted.

Welch tested the approach with GE's airplane division, which had a stated goal of reducing defects by 25 percent. Welch said that was not good enough and demanded a 70 percent reduction within three years. The bold goal "set off a chain reaction" that inspired the division to completely reimagine the entire manu-facturing process. Although the division had originally thought the stretch goal to be out of reach, it dropped the defect rate by 75 percent, achieving 3X as much as originally planned.

"Numerous academic studies have examined the impact of stretch goals," Duhigg writes, "and have consistently found that forcing people to commit to ambitious, seemingly out-of-reach objectives can spark outsized jumps in innovation and productivity."

When rethinking your marketing goals, be audacious and consider using "bullet train thinking." Obviously, this is in apparent conflict with the "Achievable" aspect of SMART goals, yet on closer inspection it is with the marrying of SMART goals with stretch goals as suggested by Duhigg that you continually tackle achievable smaller goals that make the larger goals more realistic. The stretch goals ensure the SMART goals work harder towards a more ambitious end, while the incremental SMART goals ensure that the stretch goals are actually attainable.

Another benefit of stretch goals is that the more ambitious the goal, the fewer the competitors. In *The N-Effect: More Competitors, Less Competition* by Stephen M. Garcia of the University of Michigan and Avishalom Tor of the University of Haifa, studies of students found that the fewer the perceived competitors, the greater the motivation of the student to compete and achieve.[22] The level of competition is higher for realistic goals. The advantage of setting more ambitious goals therefore includes less competition with greater effort. The combination can make it much more likely to succeed. The study may be focused on students, but really it is more about human behavior, and so is applicable to marketing teams in the same way.

Importance Of A Feedback Loop

For goals to be effective, you need feedback that reveals progress in relation to your goals. The "boxing vs. basketball" analogy illustrates the power of feedback to performance. If you do not know how you are doing, you will find it difficult or impossible to adjust the level or direction of your effort or to adapt your performance strategies to match what the goal requires.

Researchers Tamao Matsui, Akinori Okada, and Osamu Inoshita have found that, for example, if the goal is to cut down 30 trees in a day, you have no way to tell if you are on target unless you know how many trees have already been cut. When people find they are below target, they normally increase their effort or try a new strategy. The researchers concluded that summary feedback is valuable to goal achievement in that the combination of goals plus feedback is more effective than goal setting alone.[23]

In her book 9 *Things Successful People Do Differently,* Dr. Heidi Grant Halvorson, insists it is impossible to stay motivated without feedback.[24]

"We subconsciously tune in to the presence of a discrepancy between where we are now and where we want to be," writes Halvorson, the Associate Director of the Motivation Science Center at Columbia University and Senior Scientist for the Neuroleadership Institute. "When your brain detects a discrepancy, it reacts by throwing resources at it: attention, effort, deeper processing of information, and will power."

She goes on to say that without feedback, you do not know how you are doing, the discrepancy between current state and the goal is not clear, and as a result motivation is diminished, "if not wiped out altogether."

"It's the discrepancy that signals that an action is needed," Halvorson writes. "Without a discrepancy, nothing happens."

You Need A Plan

Once your marketing goals are crystal clear, you should develop a detailed action plan to achieve them. Having marketing goals without a plan is the equivalent of running your marketing on the basis of hope, which results in randomness, lack of focus, and inconsistency. It also results in a great deal of wasted time and running around in circles.

Document your goals so that there is no ambiguity in what your team is striving to achieve. Then document the execution plan for achieving your goals, and make all of this easily accessible by the team. Make it a breathing, visible set of strategies, guidelines, and tasks that your people can rely on to stay on track.

Create and maintain a shared, online marketing calendar that clarifies tasks, each task owner, and each task deadline. At our agency, we share multiple online calendars, with some covering higher-level views and others breaking down marketing categories, specific ongoing initiatives, or specific projects with highly detailed tasks. Some of our shared calendars are annual in nature, whereas others are quarterly, monthly, or weekly. A key ingredient in driving growth through marketing goals is becoming exceptional at scheduling. Once you become obsessed with your schedules, you will see how much more your team achieves.

As we have noted before, what gets measured gets done, so establish appropriate metrics for each element of the plan. Define clear success metrics and milestones. Without metrics, it is much too easy for the team to be "busy," without achieving what is important. Apply metrics and measure everything you do as a marketer, not just in terms of the marketing initiatives and campaigns themselves, but also of your team's activities and performance.

Chapter Summary

What are your top goals for the next year? Have you developed audacious goals coupled with incremental, enabling SMART goals?

Are your goals documented?

No more than three major goals at any time?

Clearly communicated to all staff?

Feedback loop in place as to progress towards goal achievement?

Let goal management empower your team to achieve more than ever before, as you rethink your marketing.

- What are your one-year, two-year, and three-year goals?
- What are your weekly, monthly, and quarterly SMART targets?
- Have you documented and clearly articulated your goals to your team? Has the team bought in?
- Have you narrowed your focus? Have you limited the number of core goals to no more than three?
- Are you actively saying "No" to anything outside of your top goals?
- Are your goals compulsory? Or "nice-to-haves"?
- Does executive management's focus meander every few months?
- Do you have a feedback loop in place to report on progress?
- Have you staffed and funded the effort sufficiently, and clarified a leader with full accountability?
- Do you have a clear deadline for each of your goals?

4

RETHINK YOUR MARKETING MIX

O h, about $30,000, $40,000, or even more.

That is the approximate investment made in a single conference and trade show by a digital marketing agency at which I used to work. The events would have 3,000 to 5,000 attendees and dozens of exhibitor booths. At one conference, I counted more than 100 booths. Competitor after competitor after competitor would line up next to one another, all targeting the same attendees. We would exhibit at these types of shows throughout the year. The annual costs totaled hundreds of thousands of dollars.

When I joined the agency, I found a good deal to like about the large events. I was able to meet people, stay up-to-date on the latest technology developments in the industry, and have the opportunity to ask questions directly to an audience that was full of potential clients. Sure enough, we would win an account or two after each event.

During a break at one of the events, I started walking down the exhibitor hall and passed a long progression of competitors' booths. They were all roughly the same – each one just another brick in the wall. Each message was a variation of the same theme. The next aisle provided the same experience. Each of the booths had brochures and datasheets, accompanied by branded coffee mugs, t-shirts, and water bottles prominently displayed as if their pile of swag was somehow special.

I quickly came to the realization that we were just one more drop in a sea of sameness. I was deeply entrenched in the industry, and even I could see that the differences among most of the agencies were only subtle.

It struck me at that moment that attendees, no matter how much they may have enjoyed a conversation at our booth, probably would have a difficult time a few weeks later separating the interaction with us from the dozens of other similar conversations in which they had engaged.

In nine years, the agency had grown to 85 employees. Without a doubt, those large conferences helped to drive that growth. Event attendance was a sizable percentage of our marketing mix at the time.

Founded in Boston, the company then opened a second office in Chicago. It then hit me. As Felonius Gru liked to say in the animated movie *Despicable Me* when he hit on a big new idea, "Light buuuuuuuuulb!"

The purpose of having a second location is to be closer to clients and prospects. Well, in that case, I thought, we should create opportunities to meet folks right there in Chicago. We were already exhibiting at large conferences there each year as was much of our competition. But only a few of our main competitors had an office in Chicago. Would it not make sense, then, to have our own branded events in Chicago where we could meet with prospects when our competitors could not? Also, if we were to host our own events, we could easily do it at less than one-tenth the cost of attending a large conference.

Light buuuuuuuuulb!

I discussed the situation with the new Managing Director of the Chicago office, and we both agreed that we should host our own exclusive local events closed to all competitors. We held our first event in a room at the House of Blues in Chicago, brought in a speaker from Google, offered awesome food and unlimited drinks. Only 10 prospective clients attended, which doesn't sound like much. The key to your marketing success, though, is not just the number of people you reach but instead is the impact your initiatives have on your business. Understanding this difference is critical if you are seeking growth.

Even though the number of attendees was limited, one attendee turned into a multi-million dollar contract – which was close to 7X larger than our average contract. A second attendee awarded us a nifty six-figure contract. Although the event was much smaller than any of the larger conferences, we realized millions of dollars in new business. We then held another event at Microsoft. Again, we landed a multi-million dollar deal with one of the attendees.

Hmm, no competitor booths lining the exhibit hall. No throngs of competitors swirling around the conference. No competitors speaking on stage. Instead, agreements worth 7X the typical contract value and secured at less than one-tenth the cost.

The local event idea caught fire, and we turned it into a road-show, hosting micro events in target cities around the country. In less than 12 months, the local events became the number one leads driver for the company.

Conventional thinking would be that hosting small groups of people at a local event should never work as effectively as getting in front of 3,000 or 5,000 people at a large conference. The numbers just do not make sense. Rethinking your marketing to unleash rapid growth, though, means testing your long-held assumptions.

While planning for that initial event in Chicago, an experienced marketer I knew warned me that it would never work. He said that people were too busy. That people had too many other event options. That no one would show up.

That is exactly the type of "been there, done that, won't work" thinking to test. Why? Because if experienced marketers across the industry are thinking like that, then your competition at that level will be zero. At the time we began running our exclusive events, no other direct competitors were doing anything similar as far as we were aware. By being the first in our space to conduct local events, we were able to stand out and capture our audience's attention.

Even though the large conferences boasted high numbers, many marketers were not able to attend because of lack of budget. We were able to offer those people a unique opportunity to gather, meet marketing peers, and talk directly with a representative from Google, Microsoft, or other industry speakers to learn about new innovations and the future direction of the industry. All at no cost to them.

We really listened to what our attendees had to say, and we made them feel special. We did not bombard them with sales pitches but instead provided them with a smaller scale version of what they would get at the larger conferences. Because of the smaller numbers, we could target our approach to their specific needs, making the event even more relevant for them. It was a unique environment, presenting attendees with many benefits and zero drawbacks.

How significant was this shift in marketing for the agency? When I joined the firm, I was the 85th employee. When I left five years later, the agency had more than 700 employees. By any measure, that is explosive growth.

You may feel your business is cruising along, growing at a steady pace, and there is nothing more you can do to spur growth. But if you truly want to get to another level, it may be time to rethink your marketing mix and methods. In our case, we had been content relying on large conferences and trade shows for leads, just like our main competitors. Instead, by rethinking our approach and hosting our own smaller, more intimate events, our leads increased, we landed many six- and seven-figure deals, and we grew our agency substantially.

When You Are Stuck, Change

Companies use a wide range of marketing tools to drive awareness, traffic, engagement, registrations, downloads, leads, and sales. Your marketing mix and methods are critical to achieving your organizational goals. You may be exhibiting at large industry conferences, as my prior employer had done. Or, you may be doing print advertising, online advertising, search advertising, native advertising, remarketing, or retargeting. Or, perhaps you are doing PR, partnerships, SEO, content marketing, product placement, custom landing pages, A/B testing, behavioral analysis, or conversion optimization.

No specific marketing vehicle is inherently better than another. The mix you choose depends on your audience, their goals, their needs, their frustrations, as well as your offering, competition, culture, and values.

If your business is stuck and growth has stalled, doing the same thing you have done in the past is not going to get you where you need to go. As Albert Einstein is believed to have said, "Insanity is doing the same thing over and over and expecting different results."

Although it may be easy and comfortable to continue doing what you have done in the past, that will likely lead you to a dead end. If you feel that in your specific industry a certain type of marketing is simply required, and that everyone in your industry does it and therefore you must do it as well, stop and reconsider. Changing your approach can make the difference between the success and failure of your marketing program.

It does not take an Einstein to realize that change is often a necessary ingredient in unleashing growth. Yet, look at marketing team after marketing team, and what do they do? They mostly do the same things year in and year out. They continue to copy competitors. Sure, they add or subtract an item to the marketing plan or make an incremental adjustment here or there, but overall the mix and methods at many companies remain mostly the same year to year.

Tinkering does not unleash growth. Tinkering leads to frustration.

Radical change unleashes growth. When you modify your marketing, flip it on its head!

If being stuck on a plateau is not an urgent problem you want to solve, tinker. If you are ready to unleash massive growth for your business, though, rethink your marketing mix and methods. It is a necessary step if you want to achieve a different, better outcome. It all starts with radical change.

Marketing Outrageously

Have you ever seen a sumo wrestler dunk a basketball? Neither had other basketball fans until the NBA's Nets (at that time playing off exit 16W in New Jersey) rethought what a professional basketball game experience should offer fans.

Jon Spoelstra, president of the Nets at the time, rethought everything the organization was doing to spur interest in the community and demonstrated a highly creative approach to transforming the team's marketing. He started by taking the traditional NBA marketing formula and tossing it out the window.

Spoelstra's marketing innovations revolutionized NBA marketing, and it has never been the same since. While he was in charge, Nets' annual ticket sales increased from $5 million to $17 million. Sponsorship fees grew from a paltry $400,000 to a robust $7 million. In total, thanks to Spoelstra's marketing genius, overall revenue rose by almost 500 percent in just three years.[1]

Spoelstra took over during the 1990's, when the Nets were a pathetic team racking up loss after loss, when player salaries were skyrocketing, and when there was no such thing as a true Nets fan. The organization was losing $4 to $5 million per season and the team had the worst record and lowest attendance of any NBA team for five straight years. Blech!

The owners discounted ticket prices and even tried giving tickets away for free. Nothing worked.

Enter Spoelstra. He outlined some of the highly unusual strategies he developed in his book *Marketing Outrageously*. Other teams marketed their own players. Spoelstra did the unthinkable at the time, and started marketing the *other team's players*. He put together ticket packages that allowed fans to see the NBA's best – Michael Jordan, Larry Bird, and Magic Johnson – and that finally got the home crowd coming back to games. He did not bother marketing his own Nets players since he already knew that was not enough of a draw.

For games against opposing teams that lacked any true star power, he came up with alternative ideas like his White Castle package – where a family of four could have dinner at White Castle and then attend the game all for an incredible $40. The White Castle nights consistently sold out.

He decided to completely ignore Manhattan and its millions of potential fans. It was thought at the time that a team in New Jersey could not survive without fans from New York City. In reality, the Nets had tried in vain for years to get New Yorkers interested in supporting the Nets, but folks in Manhattan already had a team – the New York Knicks. Why in the world would they head across the river to cheer on a team that lost most of its games?

He also stopped marketing the games themselves and focused on making them family entertainment events. Whatever happened on the court – a win or a loss – was largely irrelevant. He used huge Hollywood-style search lights. At the end of the national anthem, fireworks exploded in the building (unheard of back then). He did whatever he could to keep the crowd entertained during every stoppage of play. During timeouts in the second half of games, two huge guys in sumo wrestling outfits ran up and down the court playing basketball. According to

Spoelstra's account, they were more popular than the Nets players!

Many of these innovations have been adopted by teams throughout the league. Well, maybe not sumo wrestlers, but most of the rest.

Spoelstra even tried to rename the team the New Jersey Swamp Dragons, something he felt would get fans emotionally involved instead of a personality-less name like the Nets. Spoelstra joked that naming a basketball team the Nets was the equivalent of naming the Yankees the New York Second Bases. He wanted a name and cartoon logo that meant something and appealed especially to kids. This particular idea never made it past the owners, but it is another example of his rethinking of the team's marketing.

Spoelstra reimagined marketing for other NBA teams besides the Nets, as well. When he worked for the Sacramento Kings, ticket renewals were falling off a cliff. So, what did Spoelstra do? He took a rubber chicken wearing a jersey emblazoned with "Don't Fowl Out!" written on it, tied the chicken to a letter asking fans to renew, and stuffed everything inside a FedEx tube. The $12,000 campaign generated approximately $2.5 million in additional renewals for the team, in addition to a mountain of free publicity.

Sometimes you need to rethink your marketing mix and methods. Sometimes you need outrageous marketing. And yes, sometimes, you need dunking sumo wrestlers.

Becoming One Of The Beefiest Brands

Speaking of outrageous marketing, how would you feel if a

sandwich brand launched a hotline, offering to save vegetarians from their deep, carnivorous desires?

"Are You a Struggling Vegetarian? It can happen to anyone. One day you're a tofu-carrying vegetarian, and the next, Arby's releases Brown Sugar Bacon, making you reconsider your herbivore lifestyle. Call 1-855-MEAT-HLP to help gain control of those carnivorous impulses."

This is what was written in the Arby's Vegetarian Hotline website. The idea fell directly in line with new CMO Rob Lynch's attitude that, with a budget less than a tenth of its competitors, the brand needed to transform in a bold way. It needed to be as non-corporate as possible. It needed to resonate, especially with millennials, in a fun and authentic way. Lynch therefore decided to shake things up. Big time.

Soon after arriving at Arby's, Lynch realized that the brand had been fragmented and lost its way. The brand was being driven mostly by local store efforts, with little national guidance or coordination. The customer base was aging, fast. In fact, Arby's had the second oldest customer base in the industry at the time. And the business was floundering.

"Our customers were not loving Arby's for a very long time," Lynch revealed at the ANA Masters of Marketing Annual Conference in Orlando. In his presentation, he reported that the average annual loss per restaurant hovered around $150,000.

Lynch first re-centered the brand on its core: MEAT. He moved away from local marketing and turned to national campaigns, starting with a social listening initiative. Using the information collected, he made some key decisions and rolled out new marketing initiatives across TV, digital, social media, and public relations with a message of pure love. Love of meat, that is.

The brand has gone downright silly on social media. An actual Arby's tweet read, "We love animals... on sandwiches."

Comedian Jon Stewart used to say the harshest things about the brand on TV. Instead of having its lawyers hit him with a cease and desist letter, the company playfully engaged with Stewart, sending him and his staff free lunch after each public beatdown. When Stewart announced his retirement from The Daily Show, Arby's tweeted him a link to its "Careers" page. Timed to Stewart's final show, Arby's launched a pair of videos reminiscing about all of Stewart's attacks on the brand, set to the theme of *The Golden Girls* television show. Arby's fans gobbled it all up.

The brand launched a major campaign called "We Have The Meats" celebrating the meat stuffed inside its sandwiches. Through the brand's new social monitoring channels, the company noticed that musician Pharrell Williams was wearing the type of hat featured in Arby's logo. It engaged in a funny back-and-forth with him, requesting that he "return" Arby's hat. This drove 90,000 retweets within 12 hours and ultimately led to Pharrell listing the hat on eBay and suggesting that Arby's buy it back. Arby's paid over $44,000 for it, with all the money going to charity.

The brand launched a sponsorship of professional golfer Andrew Johnson, whose nickname is "Beef." Besides the standard sponsorship deal to sport the Arby's logo on his shirt and hat, Beef agreed to work behind the counter at an Arby's and document the entire adventure on social media.

In addition to these innovative campaigns, the company embarked on a marketing-driven revamp of the menu and an aggressive remodeling effort to make the in-store experience more pleasurable.

But it was not all fun and games for Arby's. The company got serious and raised more than $21 million dollars for the No Kid Hungry organization, dedicated to eradicating childhood hunger in the United States. Even a clown can add charity to its marketing mix.

Was marketing outrageously worth it? Arby's recently announced record annual sales of $3.6 billion, with same-store sales growth in each of the past 26 quarters and with performance over the industry average for 17 consecutive quarters. Now those are some meaty returns![2]

Simple Changes

When you rethink your marketing mix, you need to go bold but that does not mean you need to be outrageous, as Spoelstra was with the NBA or as Lynch was with Arby's. Sometimes, simply changing the marketing vehicle is what your brand needs in order to gain traction.

Hotmail was an early entrant in the web-based email market. At first it tried marketing through print ads, billboards, and other traditional approaches.

Finally, the team added the text "This email sent from Hotmail. Get your free account at Hotmail.com. P.S. I love you." at the bottom of every Hotmail email that was sent out, and linked the text to a Hotmail sign-up form. This meant that everyone receiving an email from a friend, family member, or fellow worker who was using the service would be hit with the recommendation to create an account. That one change in the marketing mix was all it took. Within six months Hotmail exploded to 1 million users. Hotmail was later purchased by Microsoft for an estimated $400 million.

Dr. Kathy Fields and Dr. Katie Rodan experienced a similar type of growth after making one major change to their marketing. The two dermatologists had created an anti-acne cream due to their frustration at the lack of new acne treatments available in the market. The approach to fighting pimples at the time – applying a cream to an individual pimple after it appeared – did not make sense to the doctors. Fields stated that it would be the equivalent of a dentist telling clients to brush only teeth with a cavity.

The two created a new treatment called Proactiv, yet had trouble making sales. They were doctors, after all, not businesspeople. They struggled for five years and essentially did not get anywhere. They tried pitching their treatment to Neutrogena, but failed. Of note during the pitch, though, Neutrogena's President, Allan Kurtzman, advised them that the product should be sold through infomercials.

The two Stanford grads were horrified, feeling much too educated and sophisticated to consider such a lowly form of marketing. However, that idea would eventually change their fortunes.

They were later introduced to the co-founder of infomercial company Guthy-Renker, and were convinced to license the product to the firm. Guthy-Renker took full responsibility for marketing. Through the use of endorsements by celebrities such as Avril Lavigne, Jessica Simpson, Katy Perry, Justin Bieber, and Vanessa Williams in the infomercials, sales took off.

The infomercials were a massive hit, helping Proactiv to become one of Guthy-Renker's most successful products, delivering approximately $1 billion in revenue in 2015.[3] Sometimes a struggling brand simply needs a new marketing vehicle.

Another example of producing explosive marketing results through a simple, yet decisive, change to the marketing mix is Moz, the web design shop turned SEO consultancy turned SEO software company.

Founder Rand Fishkin, introduced to you in the *Rethink Your Goals* chapter, walked me through some of Moz's early growth on its way towards $42.6 million in annual revenue: "In 2009, we launched our first ever email marketing campaign, where we offered a trial of the first month of our Pro subscription for $1 (we didn't have a free trial back then). That campaign was accompanied by a change to our landing page design, and in combination, they helped propel the business' revenue and customer growth massively. We went from a run rate of ~$1.5mm/year to a run rate of nearly $3mm/year overnight.

"I think that initiative was particularly effective because of the methodology behind it," Fishkin explained. "We talked to real customers and real potential customers about what made them sign up or what prevented them from signing up, and we used what we heard to craft effective messaging."

As Hotmail, Proactiv, and Moz discovered, even a single change to the marketing mix can have major ramifications to growth, regardless of whether it is a note in the footer of an email or a celebrity washing away pimples in an infomercial or the introduction of email marketing.

Growth From 10X Content Production

Hotmail, Proactiv, and Moz are all examples where one addition to the marketing mix led to significant growth. When you rethink your marketing mix, though, sometimes you need to go all-in on something you are already doing, 10X it, and transform it into a much larger slice of the marketing pie.

Mary Ellen Dugan, CMO at WP Engine (introduced to you earlier), told me of a change to WP Engine's marketing mix that continues to produce results for the WordPress hosting service, which has grown to support more than 500,000 domains.

"Over the past few years WP Engine has made a strong push into content marketing and thought leadership," Dugan told me. "We have increased our white paper and eBook production by 10X over the past two years. For example, we have an editorially independent online publication called Torque, which provides in depth insights into topical issues, technology and trends for the WordPress community. We plan to extend our overall content marketing strategy by adding new subject matter expertise, as well as unique distribution through video, social, and other content vehicles."

Further segmenting WP Engine's content strategy, the hosting company launched Velocitize, an online publication providing insights for digital marketers and agencies with strategic, open source-related insights. The site is aimed at guiding agencies and marketers through digital transformation to improve their business strategy.

By layering Velocitize onto its content marketing stack, Duggan shows she realizes that updating one's marketing mix and methods is not a one-and-done proposition. It is something that must be revisited repeatedly and aligned to the evolution of your market and customer expectations.

In an interview with DMN, Dugan further explained her approach to content marketing: "Content is most definitely still king, but it just looks different today. And in our digitized, connected world, content is pervasive. But it's clear that consumers still want to discover and be delighted. Brands and publishers need to continually rethink their content strategies to take advantage of the latest technologies and trends, and technology companies need to continue to push the boundaries of what's possible and create the infrastructure to support these new approaches.

"Some of the trends we're seeing emerge are things like personalized content at scale, co-creation of content or user-generated content, and signal-driven content," Dugan continued.[4]

Dugan further shared her thoughts with me on continually rethinking one's marketing. "As we expand globally and add new customers and industries, we need to advance our marketing approach. As we grow, we have expanded our social footprint and paid media. We are pushing to develop more thought leadership for the community and expand our mindshare through public relations as well as content development..."

WP Engine could have been comfortable cruising along with a certain level of growth. Instead, it made the commitment to a 10X increase in content production, powering its growth from 40,000 to 60,000 customers in the past year alone. With such a radical commitment to go all-in on content marketing, WP Engine is well positioned to continue strong growth into the future.

Making The Marketing Mix Legendary

Even if you want to shake up your marketing mix, the question is, where do you start and how do you know what changes to make?

One effective strategy for rethinking your mix is to break everything down into segmented analytics, and to let the numbers reveal the optimal mix. A metrics-driven approach can point you to the changes and adjustments needed to maximize your revenue.

Founded in the year 2000, Legendary Entertainment is a media company that produces movies and TV shows. Its films include *42*, *Jurassic World*, *Steve Jobs*, *Straight Outta Compton*, *Man of Steel*, *Godzilla*, and *The Hangover* series.

It is also a company that uses an astrophysicist to gain a competitive advantage.

When you think of movies, what immediately comes to mind are the traditional studios with long histories such as Universal, Paramount, and Disney. From a marketing perspective, though, the media company to watch, the one rethinking its marketing and shaking up the industry, and the one paving the path for the future, is actually Legendary. Where marketing in the movie industry has historically been done based largely on gut feeling with rudimentary audience targeting, Legendary decided to shake things up a few years ago and took a data-driven approach that is now upending the industry.

"Legendary's Applied Analytics division was established to identify efficiencies in marketing while achieving box office revenue goals," Michelle Stern, SVP of Services at Legendary, explained to me. "Something as small as a 15 percent cut in a film's media budget can save millions of dollars. More importantly, we've been able to make that reduced spend much more efficient through targeting."

The Legendary Applied Analytics division uses data analytics to create more effective and efficient digital marketing. The group, formed with the acquisition of the analytics software company StratBridge, has refined audience identification and understanding beyond what the traditional studios were ever able to achieve. The team included a Harvard astrophysicist and experts in dynamic pricing of the airline industry.[5] According to the StratBridge website, the division uses "emerging data sets to quantitatively model, predict, and influence consumer purchasing decisions" for Legendary's films, TV programs, web, and comic assets.

"One of the initial changes we made," said Stern, "was with respect to our media mix where we reallocated a portion of our budget for traditional marketing (TV, outdoor, etc.) to addressable media. We of course continue to spend meaningful amounts on broad-based channels, like TV, but we ensure that we're targeting, reaching, and engaging specific audiences beyond demographics, which we can do so well on digital channels. This is innovative in Hollywood, where the norm is to target based on four quadrants: males older than 25, males younger than 25, females older than 25, and females younger than 25."

Legendary divides these four quadrants into *millions* of groups of segments, and then analyzes each group's profile related to its movie consumption habits.[6]

"When marketing online, Legendary tests several permutations of creatives and audiences early on," Stern continued. "Think of this as small spend against several mini-campaigns to determine which creative and messaging resonate with which micro-targeted audience. Once we have this insight, we go full force on the winning combinations.

"Hollywood marketing is known for its history of 'spraying and praying' to reach relevant audiences," she explained. "Since the

Applied Analytics group was formed within Legendary, we test a multitude of micro audiences and then capitalize on what works well and cut back on what's not performing.

"We create these highly targeted audiences from multiple data sources we buy and curate, and continue to invest in and refine our data so that we can more effectively target. We first start out by targeting individuals we believe have the highest propensity to be persuaded to see our film. Targeting the persuadable set garners efficiencies in that we don't waste money on people who likely won't see the film as well as fans who already plan on seeing the movie.

"In addition to targeting individuals, we advertise to people who have interests or behaviors likely to correlate with the type of person who will want to see the film," Stern said. "This is where our analytics competencies come into play – our data science team develops tools that enable us to identify actionable insights. Many of these interests are obvious – like genre-specific interests that match the film – but about 20 percent aren't obvious and must be gleaned by data analysis. For instance, we learned when marketing the Godzilla film that fans of the movie happen to like the Toyota brand. That enabled us to find more lookalikes of Godzilla fans based on that characteristic and others."

Rethinking marketing in the entertainment industry has given Legendary a strategic competitive advantage while strengthening the firm's financials. The success was so impressive that in 2016, the Chinese conglomerate Wanda Group purchased Legendary for $3.5 billion, the largest deal of its kind ever in China.[7]

If you are unsure what to change in your marketing mix, follow

Legendary's lead and dive into your analytics to provide direction. Hiring a Harvard astrophysicist to help you is optional.

Rethinking The Blender

Legendary was highly structured and focused when rethinking its marketing mix and methods. Sometimes, though, simply having your eyes and ears open will help you to be opportunistic and pounce on an idea if it looks enticing enough.

As a child, Tom Dickson was addicted to innovation. He rigged his doorbell to open the front gate. He configured go-karts with engines that traveled faster than 80 miles per hour.

So, it was no surprise that George Wright, the new Marketing Director at Blendtec, an unknown blender manufacturing company that Dickson founded, stumbled upon Dickson in the factory working on a blender one day. What took Wright by surprise was the sawdust and wood shavings on the floor next to Dickson's workbench. Wright walked into the company's founder testing changes to a blender by grinding up a 2x2. Apparently, this was not an uncommon sight in the factory.

Wright was wrestling with a tiny marketing budget, as the company preferred to spend its money on engineering and design. Brand awareness was practically nonexistent, and Wright did not have the budget to change that.

Or did he?

Taking in the scene, Wright realized the powerful visual in front of him and decided to turn it into a video series called "Will It Blend?" The videos featured Dickson – clad in a scientist's white lab coat – conducting tests of everyday objects to confirm if they could be ground up using a Blendtec blender. The initial five videos cost $50, including the cost of the lab coat, the website domain, and the blending targets – a garden rake, a rotisserie chicken, and a Big Mac Extra Value Meal.

The initial "Will It Blend?" videos were posted online in October of 2006, and within five days had attracted over six million views. As the video series continued, Dickson blended an iPhone, iPad, Rubik's Cube, Wii remote, tire repair kit, marbles, golf balls, crowbar, and many other items. In total, the videos have been viewed over 100 million times and Dickson has been featured on The Today Show, The Tonight Show, The History Channel, and others.

Within a year and a half of posting the videos, consumer sales increased 700 percent. In addition, Blendtec was able to generate incremental revenue streams from paid speaking engagements and revenue-sharing checks from video sites such as YouTube.[8]

The "Will It Blend?" series works for many reasons. It truly is remarkable what the product can chop to bits. It is an authentic demonstration of the product's power. It is surprising and memorable. It gives a face and personality to the brand. Plus, it is just plain fun and makes you not only smile, but also makes you want to tell others about it.

The Blendtec video series is literally a case of being opportunistic on the way to rethinking the marketing "mix." Get it? (I know, I know, I can already hear my kids groaning at me...)

Being Opportunistic On The Way To Capturing One-Third Of The Fortune 100

Another example of being opportunistic is Affectiva, an emotion AI technology company spun out of the MIT Media Lab. In

Affectiva's case, although it had never focused on PR in the past, an article in The New Yorker changed that in a big way. Raffi Khatchadourian, staff writer at The New Yorker, wrote an extensive piece (close to 8,000 words) in 2015 on Affectiva and Co-founder/CEO Rana el Kaliouby.[9] The effort took a full three months. And it appears that the time was well worth it.

As CMO Gabi Zijderveld explained to me, the article was a total game changer for the business and made Affectiva shift its marketing focus to PR. Not only did the article bring in new leads for Affectiva, it helped educate prospective clients about the new world of emotion recognition technology. Affectiva was hooked on PR. Following the New Yorker piece, the media outlets covering Affectiva included Bloomberg, CBS, CNN, Forbes, Fortune, Inc., PBS NewsHour, PC Magazine, Tech-Crunch, VentureBeat, Wired, among others.

As a result, Affectiva exploded with growth and now has approximately one-third of the Fortune 100 as clients. Its client base overall extends across 75 countries. From movie studios testing promos and trailers, to brands testing reactions to their ads, to computer game developers adapting game play to players' emotional states, Affectiva has organizations from various industries reaching out to explore the possibilities of its emotion analytics solutions. And it has a shift in its marketing mix largely to thank for that.

Hurdling Over Obstacles On The Path To Growth

No matter what you decide to change in your marketing mix, realize that you may need to change it again and again and again over time.

To understand the power of continual marketing mix evolution, let us go back to May 2, 2010, which in many ways was just another day. Except, on that day, 4,500 adventurous pioneers charged through seven miles of mud and countless obstacles in Macungie, Pennsylvania en route to the first-ever Tough Mudder finish line. With obstacles ranging from "Electroshock Therapy" to "Arctic Enema" and "Berlin Walls," the hardcore obstacle course event has rapidly grown in popularity, earning more than $100 million in revenue in just its fifth year.[10]

Approximately 500,000 people complete marathons and 1.4 million run in half-marathons every year. Tough Mudder's founders, Will Dean and Guy Livingstone, felt that many people found these long-distance runs boring. They also felt marathons were poorly organized and operated. They therefore saw this as an opportunity for a bit of a revolution in the endurance sports industry.

In the beginning, Tough Mudder relied on a measly $8,000 budget and Facebook ads to spread its message. It then turned to organic sharing on social media. Then came an all-in approach to video. In 2012, the company produced approximately 47 YouTube videos, a 176 percent increase over the prior year's number and a 4,600 percent increase in two years.

In 2014, it shifted the strategy again. Where the early videos focused on event recaps, the new videos highlighted new obstacles and inspirational participants.

"Our highest-performing type of content, short videos on YouTube and Facebook, capture the spirit of our events, as well as the inspiring stories of our participants," Jerome Hiquet, Tough Mudder's CMO, explained to me. Hiquet felt that video was a perfect medium for Tough Mudder, because although photos can be effective in the marketing mix, for something as unique as Tough Mudder you really needed video to convey an experience that includes mud, ice, fire, and even electrical shocks. Tough Mudder now uses video throughout the marketing funnel.

In an interview on CMO.com, Hiquet further detailed the brand's commitment to video: "We knew that the content from our events could be a very strong and powerful tool that we should leverage much more, not only by using it for PR stories in traditional media, but also by leveraging the events as an opportunity to engage our database and our customers. So we decided to live-stream our event through multiple platforms—Facebook Live, the website, and Periscope. During our second event of the year [2016] in the U.S., we saw huge reach and engagement. In two days, we reached more than 7 million people. We had more than 1.5 million video views. We had more than 300,000 engagements through social media. It's clearly a way to maintain engagement within the community but also reach new people who don't necessarily know Tough Mudder or could be scared about doing a Tough Mudder, and show them what you experience and the values behind that."[11]

"We use video across the entire marketing funnel," Hiquet said in a Marketing Land interview, "both to introduce the event to people who have never heard of it (for example, through pre-roll ads on YouTube), then as a mid-funnel entertainment device to energize and inspire our five million-plus global Facebook community, and finally as a bottom-funnel tool on our website to highlight our innovative obstacles and showcase inspirational participant stories.

"Over time we've been getting shorter and shorter," he continued. "These days our average videos are under the two-minute mark, although it does vary... On the other hand, we've done a 15-minute documentary of our 24-hour non-stop event called

World's Toughest Mudder. This month we are releasing a 5-part mini-documentary series called 'Obstacles Redefined' about our internal obstacle innovation team. It's pretty eye-opening."[12]

Through the years, video helped to drive the company's growth. As the obstacle course industry now fights through its first stage of saturation, though, Tough Mudder is rethinking its marketing mix and methods again for what it sees as a path to future growth and greater influence. To Hiquet, that means new partnerships, TV broadcasting, and a switch to a mobile-first mindset.

In gazing into the crystal ball of Tough Mudder's future, Hiquet filled me in on the brand's direction. "Over the last two years, the brand has expanded beyond its nearly 2.5 million global participants through partnerships with CBS Sports, Livestream and Merrell, and through international expansion with partnerships with IMG and Seroja," he said. "Tough Mudder's multi-year partnership with CBS brings the events to broadcast, cable and digital on CBS Sports, CBS Sports Network, and CBSSports.com. The partnership enables us to further grow our community and provides new platforms to engage with participants." The series is also being broadcast by UK TV channel Sky Sports Mix.

Beyond partnerships, the company has become mobile-first in its orientation.

"From an e-commerce standpoint, over 60% of our traffic is coming from mobile," Hiquet stated in his CMO.com interview. "We have even changed our approach since I arrived, thinking for every user experience, every communication on our platform, thinking first about mobile and then about desktop. Everything in terms of content creation, content activation, we are really thinking of how it could be specifically relevant for people who are using mobile."[13]

Tough Mudder has proven that continual evolution of the marketing mix is a highly effective strategy. Strategic partnerships. TV broadcasting. Mobile-first approach. Put it all together, and you get a brand that is endearing itself to a devoted audience that is sure to support its continued growth.

Proving There Is A Better Way

In the *Rethink Your Goals* chapter, I introduced you to the risk analytics software company Provenir. Adi Bachar-Reske, Global Head of Marketing, told me of an event marketing incident at Provenir similar to my experience at my prior employer.

According to Bachar-Reske, prior to her arrival, Provenir was a regular participant in a number of expensive trade shows. As in my experience, competitors lined the exhibit floor. The events were just not effective for Provenir.

Instead of continuing to pour money into these shows, Provenir decided to rethink its approach to events. Bachar-Reske did not want to completely abandon them, but she wanted to make them more effective.

Bachar-Reske found a way.

Rather than emptying the budget to pay for the events, Bachar-Reske decided to take a guerrilla approach. Instead of setting up a booth, Provenir bought a few passes and focused its attention on conversations with leads. To prepare, the company's inside sales team conducted extensive research prior to the event ahead of time and prescheduled meetings with specific prospects. And not just a few meetings, but as many as it could possibly jam into its schedule. At one event, the team booked a jaw-dropping 60 meetings.

Provenir meticulously tracks the results from these meetings and Bachar-Reske confirmed that this process produces significant new revenue, finally enabling Provenir to generate a strong ROI from events.

But that is only part of Provenir's rethinking story...

From Agency To Inbound

Bachar-Reske did not stop rethinking with Provenir's event marketing. She also rethought the company's approach to PR.

When Bachar-Reske joined the firm, Provenir was relying on a PR agency, which in the traditional model acted as a go-between with the company and journalists. The stories pitched by the PR agency could take six months for a publication decision by media outlets to be made. The process took much too long and delivered few results.

So Bachar-Reske rethought PR for Provenir. Instead of relying on an outside agency to try to secure media mentions and other forms of exposure, Bachar-Reske took control and brought the function in-house, launching an inbound approach to extend the reach and visibility of the company.

Provenir started focusing on content generation and distribution, and journalists started taking notice. For example, one blog post prompted three journalists to approach Provenir asking to write an article.

Much of the content Provenir creates is now shared by various publications in the industry. The company continuously pumps out byline articles for industry websites. For example, when

Bachar-Reske discovered a publication that was effective at targeting community banks, she had her team go to work on creating related content and distributing it to its list.

Provenir flipped the traditional model of gaining exposure on its head. It now has the power to attract industry notice instead of relying on a lengthy, often fruitless PR method of trying to gain attention. The inbound program has been so successful that the company has discontinued all advertising, cutting significant costs.

The business impact from these changes to Provenir's marketing? A massive increase in leads over the prior year with significant cost savings. More leads. Lower costs. Pretty cool.

Now that is rethinking one's marketing!

Upgrading The Marketing Mix And Growing 2,400 Percent

An important area to explore when looking at your marketing mix is strategic partnerships. Find other organizations already doing a great deal of business with your core audience and organizations that would greatly benefit from your involvement in fulfilling their needs. This is low-hanging fruit since partnerships can get you in front of more prospects faster. In fact, a Frost & Sullivan survey found that more CEOs pointed to strategic partnerships as their number one growth strategy than any other strategy.[14]

The ecommerce solutions company Shopify has increased its customer base by 2,400 percent in the past five years and now serves more than 325,000 merchants.[15] That's right, 2,400 percent. That is not a typo!

One of the underlying drivers of the success has been the attitude and approach of CMO Craig Miller. After assuming his new role at the software firm, he rebranded the marketing group as the growth team, aligning everyone to the specific goal of growth. In addition, Miller obsessively looked for ways to improve the onboarding process, no matter how small the enhancement. In one year, he signed up for the service 1,000 times to find ways to make the process more efficient and user friendly.

Shopify has deployed strategic partnerships as a key component of its marketing mix and an integral catalyst for business growth. In 2015, Amazon replaced its existing selling platform, allowing Shopify to provide merchant services to Amazon's third-party vendors. This alone led to a 70 percent annual increase in merchants using the Shopify platform.

The main benefit of Shopify's partnerships has been acquiring new merchants, which has resulted in dramatic increases in the company's subscription revenue. In addition, since Shopify takes a cut of every transaction on its platform, more stores means more transactions, bringing in additional revenue.

10X The Conversion Rate By Eliminating Sales Objections

As part of rethinking your marketing mix, you should review the aspects of your marketing that are deeply tied to the sales process. Yes, a sponsorship of a professional golfer named "Beef" might be effective for Arby's, but it can also be just as critical to focus on marketing elements that more directly impact your conversions at the point of sale.

That brings us to Jerome's Furniture, a 60-year-old, third-generation, family business in Southern California. The company has a robust online presence, with 75 percent of the company's traffic coming from visitors to its website. With that in mind, Jerome's decided to improve online engagement and the website experience for its audience to drive a higher conversion rate.

It implemented online chat so online customers could get immediate answers to their questions, hopefully eliminating purchase objections in the process.

An enhanced website would also provide the sales team with better insights into its audience, giving the company feedback it previously did not have. This enabled the company to streamline and improve the user experience.

Jerome added an effective twist to the new website process by having in-store staff man the chat line, instead of outsourcing the function to an outside call center. This enabled faster, more detailed responses to customer inquiries. For example, if a customer had a question about a specific piece of furniture, the Jerome employee could walk over to the piece, snap a quick photo of the area in question, and add it to the chat discussion for the caller to see immediately.

Online chat helped increase the sales conversion rate for online visitors by a whopping 1,000 percent.[16]

The lesson here is not about online chat per se. Rather, it is about looking for added marketing mix elements that you can seamlessly combine with your sales process. The more you can remove doubt and eliminate buyer objections at the point of sale in the shopping process itself, the more likely you are to increase your conversion rates.

Choosing The Right Mix

By now you should be able to see that changing your marketing mix can be a powerful way to unleash revenue growth. Doing the "same old, same old" often produces the "same old, same old" results. Or, even worse, produces weaker results. It is baffling how so many companies stick to the same formula even in the face of flat or decreasing revenue, but it is something commonly seen across many industries.

Marketing teams often believe that commonplace industry methods are non-negotiable and mandatory regardless of their overall budget. Advertising was often seen this way in the past. More recently you may have seen this attitude in regards to conference exhibits and now with social media.

Changing your marketing mix is an easy proposition. What is difficult is making the right changes – making the adjustments that will deliver significantly better results.

Where do you start? How do you determine which parts of the equation to change?

The best place to start is with subtraction. Eliminate anything that is siphoning resources away from more productive marketing vehicles. Review the results of your marketing efforts. What are the bottom 20 percent of achievers? Jettison them immediately. Many marketing teams hesitate to give up on marketing vehicles for the fear of missing opportunity. It is important to understand that subtraction is a crucial part of the process of finding the optimum marketing mix.

Subtracting ineffective components of your marketing program will free up your time, money, and other resources. To ensure every dollar of your marketing budget is going towards growth-generating activities, you should continually be transferring dollars from low-performing activities to higher achievers.

Using the following three-step process will help you properly adjust your marketing mix.

First, identify the specific objectives you wish to achieve from the changes. What metric are you expecting to change? Visibility? Website traffic? Registrations? Demo downloads? Form submissions? Media hits? Inbound calls?

More directly related to sales, are you looking to increase the number of commitments to onsite pitches? Or is your priority achieving a higher average order value? Or is your goal to achieve higher prices or increase sheer volume?

Be very clear. What specifically do you want? Without clear objectives, your efforts will be unfocused and random, an inefficient and costly outcome.

Second, outline your options and be honest about the obstacles associated with each one. For example, if you specified website traffic as your focus, you need to objectively list the challenges to increasing traffic and then determine ways to adjust your marketing mix to overcome those challenges.

You may consider SEO as a good option for driving increased traffic. Maybe you have ignored SEO or perhaps you have tried and failed at it in the past. Whatever the reason, the key is to be as detailed as possible with your action plan.

For optimizing your website for SEO, you might list the following possible marketing tactics:

- Keyword research
- Title tags and meta data optimization

- URL naming
- Competitive landscape analysis
- Technical optimization
- Ensuring that your website is mobile-friendly
- Accelerating page load speed
- Adding more rich, in-depth, and valuable content
- Blogging, with posts optimized for your target topics
- Internal linking
- Disavowing bad external links
- Adding real external links
- Integrating with other marketing channels to capture demand
- Etc.

Third, assign a difficulty ranking for each line item. How much effort, resources, time, and money would it take to tackle each of your proposed elements? Give each one a grade.

Perform this exercise for all the options you consider, whether SEO or paid search, display advertising, native advertising, print advertising, TV advertising, radio advertising, site retargeting, public relations, event marketing, content marketing, videos, podcasts, email marketing, social media, paid social, direct mail, word-of-mouth, affiliate marketing, product placement, celebrity marketing, in-store marketing, billboards, kiosks, partnerships, sponsorships, or cross-branding. Think that a sandwich board is what you need to add to your marketing mix? Add it to the list.

Compare your different options and grade them based on their potential impact to your stated objective. How much do you think it will move the needle? What is the potential? Can it scale?

With a detailed list of options complete with levels of difficulty and probable impact to your stated goals, you can begin narrowing the list to those actions that are easiest to achieve and will get you closest to your stated objectives. Anything requiring extensive effort and limited potential should be removed immediately. Discard anything that produces small results regardless of the effort. Why do it if the potential just is not there? (Perhaps you should stop spending so much time on your Snapchat account, right?)

Now, layer in urgency. How soon do you need to see results? The marketing mix that will generate results this week or this month will likely be extremely different from the measures that are likely to achieve results in a year or two. Choose the marketing vehicles that offer the greatest gains with the least amount of effort. The goal is to maximize results with the smallest possible investment.

For my prior employer, launching a roadshow with local events around the country proved to be that option. For WP Engine, a 10X increase in content marketing proved to be the right choice. For Legendary, it was a turbocharged analytics team, while for Jerome's, it was online chat.

Big potential?

Relatively low effort?

Aligned to your urgency and timing?

You have yourself a winner. Add it to your mix and start unleashing revenue growth.

Chapter Summary

If you are looking to unleash revenue growth, changing your marketing mix is a good area to explore. The addition of new components in your mix can often give your marketing just the spark you need.

Merely tinkering around the edges with your marketing mix, though, tends to cause frustration, as it rarely makes a difference. While it provides you with the feeling that you are being innovative and testing new avenues, it is often an illusion.

Brands that achieve breakthroughs and exceptional growth do so because of a *major* shift in marketing mix. Look at Blendtec and Affectiva. Look at Arby's and Tough Mudder. Look at Legendary Entertainment and Proactiv. If you want radical marketing results, then make a radical change to your marketing mix.

Be bold.

- What is your current marketing mix?
- Have you analyzed your marketing analytics in extreme detail, like Legendary Entertainment does, to identify needed changes to your marketing?
- What are the top performers in your mix?
- What are the bottom 20 percent? How quickly can you eliminate them?
- What specifically are you trying to achieve in improving your marketing results?
- What is the effort required for each component in your marketing mix? Cost? Time? Resources?
- What new options should you consider adding to the mix? What totally outrageous ideas can you brainstorm? (No, you do not need to hire basketball-playing sumo wrestlers or pay Pharrell Williams $44,000 for a hat...well, unless you want to.)
- What is the upside potential of each new option?

- How quickly will you see the results from the new option?
- Among the low effort, high return options, which are your finalists?
- Which one or two additions will you commit to and focus on?
- How will you go all-in, avoid tinkering, and produce radical results?

5

RETHINK YOUR METRICS

When I was at a previous agency, a marketing manager from a pasta manufacturer called and asked us to submit a proposal for SEO. The company's goal was to increase traffic to its website by a certain percentage.

Normally that would be a reasonable high-level goal for a consumer product goods company, which did not have any ecommerce in its website. However, a review of the brand's website revealed that the site, well... How can I put this? Well, it sucked. Boring, boring, boring.

The company had invested a great deal in videos, but each one was less compelling than the next. The videos focused on recipes – a popular concept for a food-related site – but the presentation was so dull and lifeless, I could not get all the way through any of them.

Looking into the brand's website analytics revealed that anyone getting to the site hardly ever went beyond one page per visit.

Clearly, I was not alone in thinking that the site was not worth the time.

I explained to the marketing department that SEO would be a bad idea since driving traffic to a bad brand experience would do more harm than good. And clearly, measuring visits to the site would do nothing toward improving the business.

A reset of what was important was clearly in order. The brand needed to rethink the appropriate metrics by which to measure the site's success.

At the time, fragmentation of the family was a hot topic in the media, so I pitched the marketing team on the idea of being the brand that brings the family back to the dining room table. I suggested rebranding (not just the website, but every representation and touchpoint of the brand) to make everything about bringing the family together. We would build SEO into the DNA of the campaign and a redesigned website, and *then* SEO would be a powerful force for the brand.

The brand loved the idea and started the transformation. The website was redesigned and a microsite exclusively in support of the "eating together" theme was launched. We optimized the sites and enjoyed major success. More importantly, the brand now had a platform on which to build a powerful marketing program to build a loyal fan base. The meaningful meals mission is still being espoused by the brand today, nine years later.

The pasta company's initial desire to focus on organic search traffic – getting more people to the site – was flawed. Because its website experience was so bad, an increase in traffic would have had a negative impact on the business. It needed to fix a core problem before pushing more people to the site. While measuring site visitors can be an important metric, in the case of the pasta company it was actually harmful.

When looking at how to move the needle for your business, you need to dig deep to truly understand the metrics that matter most. In the case of the pasta company, it had been completely ignoring metrics related to engagement and the customer experience (1:1 ratio of site visits to page views, high bounce rates, anemic time-on-site stats, embarrassingly low video views, zero engagement with the brand, etc.).

In this situation, the customer experience metrics pointed to something very wrong not only with the company's website, but with its branding and overall marketing. We could have worked hard on SEO on the old site, but not only would that have been a waste of time, it also would have exacerbated the problem and inflicted longer-term damage to the brand. People do not forget a bad brand experience and then reconsider the brand the next day. The real impact is that you lose these visitors for years or possibly forever. Worse, you risk them sharing their negative thoughts and feelings with others, whether through casual conversation or social media. Obviously, this would not have been a great strategy.

When I talk about rethinking your metrics, I am saying you need to ignore the standard, generic, safe metrics that almost everyone else is talking about. Instead, you need to dig deeply into your own brand, your own audience, and your own assets. What is your customers' journey? Where are the potholes? Why are they there? How can you not only fill the potholes, but also build a better road overall – one that not only "gets more traffic," but one that strengthens your brand for greater results now as well as into the future? Then you can define the metrics that would bring this about.

What really impacts your business? What distinguishes your best customers from the pack? What is the one most significant metric that makes the difference between ho hum results and sheer awesomeness? Diving into your marketing metrics is one of the key ways to uncover the underlying movers and shakers of your business.

Do not just follow the crowd. Be smarter than the crowd.

Rethinking your metrics is not just about a "measurement." It is about everything related to the business that underlies that metric, as well. Now *that* is rethinking your metrics.

The Misguided Allure Of Industry-Standard Metrics

The lesson? Know what truly drives your results.

The number of distractions you face on a daily basis can easily overwhelm you. Many of the numbers you are told are important, actually have little impact on your business.

I am not saying that standard metrics are universally bad. It should be recognized, though, that many people's inherent inclination is to be risk averse, as on a gut level they do not want to risk losing their job. Therefore, there is an allure to industry standard metrics. Sometimes measuring site traffic can be a key performance indicator that directly leads to revenue growth. For the pasta company, that was not the case. For others in certain situations, though, it certainly can be the right performance indicator.

Question your industry's standard metrics, and always ask what would produce even greater results. To achieve the amazing, you often need to rethink what everyone else in your industry believes is the right way of doing things.

Another Misguided Strategy

A different type of situation came up when the President of a billion dollar enterprise software company hauled in our client – a marketing executive – and demanded a Pinterest strategy. Pinterest was all the rage in the media at the time. It made absolutely no sense for that company in that market to waste resources on such a strategy, but our contact was unwilling to tell the President the truth. He felt compelled to come up a Pinterest strategy, albeit a pointless one.

We both knew that the brand's target audience would have no interest in looking at the brand's Pinterest boards. We both knew it would have zero effect on the business, zero effect on revenue, and zero meaning to its clients. It would waste everyone's time and divert resources away from critical marketing activities. It was purely and simply a silly exercise stemming from the media's hype machine.

When I pressed my client for the success metrics that would define the performance of the Pinterest initiatives, I was met with an awkward silence. Sadly, even if my client was measuring the number of views of its pins, it would be even more noise to distract the brand from what really mattered. I urged my client to avoid wasting time and energy on the effort.

My client went through with the initiative without any business-impacting metrics upon which to measure performance and became a perfect example of chasing the shiny new object, instead of focusing on metrics that would move the business forward. Of course, the Pinterest efforts did not bring in any new leads, nor any business results. What it did was waste time and resources. The saddest part about the story is that it is true, and that this type of mindless activity happens all too often.

Rethinking your metrics ties in directly with rethinking your strategy. If you cannot identify meaningful success metrics that have a real impact on your business, then you need to start over.

The World Is A Noisy Place

Beware of the shiny object syndrome, where you are endlessly chasing the latest hyped up marketing vehicle. Many metrics can be noise, having no real effect on driving your revenue. You may have many Facebook Followers or Instagram "Likes," but that may have no relationship to your sales and revenue.

You can easily be swallowed up by the media's hyper focus on the new things you supposedly MUST do. How your business will suffer and you will be left in the dust if you do not follow the crowd.

Speakers at industry conferences may preach that you must be a Snapchat leader or millennials will never care about your brand. Colleagues may keep asking you about your virtual reality strategy. All of this muddies the water and forces you to take your eye off what is really important: how does your brand make customers happy and grow business successfully.

I am not saying that new things are bad or that many of these innovative ideas are not important. Innovation is critical in providing you with opportunities to forge a competitive edge.

I am just saying that you can become caught up in too many different marketing activities, with some of them distracting you from what you must do to move the needle. I am saying that I have seen time and time again brands that get distracted by meaningless metrics rather than focusing like a laser on what matters most. If you want to grow fast and profitably, you need to focus on the things that truly can make a positive impact on *your* business.

You need to say "no" to most of the irrelevant "stuff" thrown your way and instead identify what is going to really make an impact. Then report on the appropriate metrics, analyze the results, and adjust, optimize, and improve religiously.

Mary Ellen Dugan at WP Engine, introduced to you earlier, clearly understands the need to focus on those things that are important and ignore those that are not.

"The best marketers will be those who can craft a strategy to stay ahead," Dugan says. "The pace of data integration and analytics is a key area that is changing rapidly and one that will continue to evolve. The goal is to learn to separate the signal from the noise and figure out what information or insights truly will drive your business forward and learn how those insights could change over time. Teams can't wait for the data scientist to pull the numbers. They need to be able to access and distill data into insights and into actions. Marketers need to get much more comfortable with data overall and blend the art and science of every marketing effort."

Rethinking The Metrics Of The National Pastime

WARP, UZR, and BABIP in baseball. Corsi and Fenwick in hockey. VORP and OWS in basketball.

Some sophisticated new techno-language? In a way, yes. It is the tip of the new statistical iceberg that has taken over decision making in sports. Big data and the technology to slice it and dice it in a myriad of ways has allowed executives in baseball, hockey, basketball, and other sports to look at things differently. Analysis and advanced metrics are now the big thing. For a good reason – they work.

No sport has been as immersed in metrics and statistics as baseball. Records go back to the 19th century and you can easily retrieve the leading batting averages, ERAs, and RBIs of the stars of the time. But even such a traditional – some would say stodgy – institution as baseball is evolving through the use of metrics.

Billy Beane, immortalized in the book and movie *Moneyball*, was one of the leading proponents of advanced metrics in baseball. Strapped by a small-market budget, the general manager of the Oakland Athletics needed to find a way to compete with his more well-heeled competitors. He found it in data, technology, and a creative use of metrics unheard of and unfamiliar to his peers.

His bevy of new metrics revealed value where no one else could see it. He was able to acquire players no one else wanted at economical prices because he identified key attributes that would allow those players to help the A's win.

The A's budget was roughly a third that of the high spenders like the Red Sox and Yankees. After the low budget A's reached the playoffs four years in a row from 2000-2003, other teams began to catch on. Big market teams like the Boston Red Sox jumped on board, hiring noted stats guru Bill James to help them utilize technology and data to improve the team. Like the A's, the Red Sox found success – building World Series champions in 2004, 2007, and 2013.

The focus on analytics and metrics has since spread to all sports, even ones like hockey where it was thought sophisticated advanced metrics would not apply. The obsession with metrics has even hit the concession stands, with certain teams using real-time metrics to determine how to sell more hot dogs and beer during games.

The lesson? Finding different metrics – ones which are relevant to your business – can help you better understand performance and provide you with a significant competitive edge.

Beane and other sports executives changed their games. You need to change yours. If you ignore the value of technology and data and choose to do things the old way, you will fall behind, be at a significant disadvantage, and start losing to your competitors who are making use of new metrics.

In marketing, we now have endless tools and technologies for everything from dynamic display advertising to content marketing, influencer marketing, site retargeting, behavioral analysis, conversion optimization testing, among many other marketing vehicles. Each comes with its own set of standard practices in the industry. Like Beane did in baseball, find the metrics that work specifically for you regardless of best practices. It will give you a leg up on your competition.

Focus On Your Audience

Sometimes focusing too much on traditional metrics can blind you from seeing what your audience really wants and from achieving larger marketing wins. What is it that your audience thinks about? What do they care about? It is typically not your product or service. It is usually all about them. Do your metrics reflect this?

During the infancy of YouTube, I was contacted by the shampoo brand of a multi-billion dollar corporation. The marketing director measured the success of the brand's digital marketing by website traffic and said he wanted to increase traffic. A look at the brand's marketing approach quickly surfaced the problem. Its content centered on the ingredients in the shampoo, which the company felt to be superior to the competition.

The problem is, no one cared.

The audience data revealed that very few people were searching for or consuming information related to shampoo ingredients. No magazines, or newspapers, or television shows were covering the topic. No one was sharing information online about it. There was simply little to no interest in shampoo ingredients.

Unfortunately, the marketing team was not aware of it. Why? Because while they were measuring website traffic, they were not collecting any metrics on what was important – or in this case what *wasn't* important – to their audience.

From my perspective, the issue was not website traffic. Just like the pasta company, the brand was measuring the wrong thing. Although with the shampoo brand it was not a case of a "bad experience" on its website. It was a simple disconnect with what mattered to its audience.

To solve the problem, two colleagues and I researched the shampoo landscape like crazy and found there were no major brands at the time focused on hairstyles. Short hairstyles, long hairstyles, curly hairstyles, hairstyles for weddings, hairstyles for a night out, prom hairstyles, bob hairstyles, voluminous long layers, twisted mohawk, double-knotted updo, chained mermaid braids, cornrow braids, side-parted lobs, Gatsby waves, disco buns, etc. The list is endless. (Who knew???) The Google search volumes for the hairstyles universe were off the charts – even higher than the search volumes for shampoo itself.

So, we suggested to the brand that before it started driving more traffic to the site, it should instead rework the brand to focus on hairstyles. When we showed the evidence of consumers' extreme interest in hairstyles, the marketing team loved the idea and completely transformed the brand. It revamped the website to focus on hairstyles and to include hairstyle how-to videos. It refocused its TV ads, print ads, digital advertising, and SEO – all with a singular focus on hairstyles. We embarked on a major outreach program to build relationships with beauty and hair blogs.

After the change, traffic to the site as well as YouTube video views, social shares, and blogger engagement with the brand increased over 10X. The campaign was so successful, the brand ran with it for years. This never would have happened had the brand continued to focus on its metrics completely divorced from a measure of customer love. Instead, we found out what the audience was craving and simply gave them what they wanted.

Make sure that in your marketing reporting, you are not simply feeding the beast. Reporting on the numbers is important, but looking at the qualitative value of the underlying conversations you are having with your audience is equally as critical. Ironically, focusing exclusively on your metrics can actually hurt your numbers. If you optimize something that they do not care about, you will get mediocre results. Instead, focus on creating brand love, and you will achieve more magical returns.

The Fulcrum And Lever

Finding the right metrics is often hard work. It is tempting to focus on certain safe, familiar metrics. Everyone understands them. Discussions about them will get lots of head nodding. No one will blame you for focusing on these metrics.

The numbers could be rocketing in the "right" direction, but there is only one problem. Revenue is not growing.

That is because you have been sidetracked by red herrings. The "safe" metrics can often be the wrong metrics. You can measure them forever, but they may not reveal what you really want to see – how to unleash massive revenue growth.

For that you have to go back to something that was discovered in ancient Greece – the power of the fulcrum and the lever. Archimedes discovered that if you have a long enough lever and a solid point from which to apply pressure to move something (the fulcrum), you can move mountains.

Your challenge is to examine your marketing program to find the fulcrum and long lever to move your boulders. What key metrics can you leverage to make exponential change?

For example, one company that came to our agency had been frustrated with its lead volume. It was convinced that it needed a larger database of prospects. When we started analyzing its website, though, what became clear was that a larger database would probably not move the needle for them. The problem for the brand was that the messaging was not speaking to the audience's pain points. In our behavioral analysis data, we found that few site visitors were clicking on the main call-to-action buttons. Deeper in the site we uncovered the information that not only attracted the most attention from site visitors but was a prerequisite for them to complete an online form – unfortunately, this information was buried in the website.

Sure, we could have spent our time exclusively focused on expanding the database, but the lever was much longer (and therefore stronger) by following the behavioral data and making corresponding design, organizational, and messaging changes in the site. Changing the underlying metrics we were examining made all the difference.

A SaaS (Software as a Service) company came to our agency focused on the lead volume from its digital advertising campaigns. The brand was focused on metrics like impressions, impression share, clicks, cost-per-click, click-through rate, and conversions, yet what the team consistently talked about was the ads and costs. The brand was inexplicably ignoring the most direct factor of the conversion rate – the landing page. We flipped the focus and centered our attention on the conversion rate. After tossing the existing landing page template aside and launching a completely new, overhauled template, conversion rates increased and consequently monthly lead volume went through the roof, ultimately improving by 140 percent within a year.

We taught our client that a high click-through rate could actually be a negative, masking underlying problems. For example, such a rate would lead to higher costs without a return when the conversion rate was extremely low. By focusing on the conversion rate, we not only had an outsized impact on lead volume but also saved a great deal of money for our client by pausing any ads with a high click-through rate yet low conversion rate. By reallocating such funds towards ads with high conversion rates, our results were compounded.

Facebook is another case of rethinking metrics for growth. Facebook has continually examined its user behavior in an effort to increase user activity on its platform, identifying what it calls North Star metrics and then focusing its attention on driving growth accordingly. According to Chamath Palihapitiya, who had been VP of User Growth, Mobile, and International while at Facebook, the company at one time had recognized that many new users would use the platform once, and then never return. In analyzing the data of these types of users and comparing it against those who stuck around and used the site extensively, the Facebook team identified that getting to seven friends in 10 days was the key to greatly increasing user retention and engagement. Once this epiphany occurred, Facebook focused like a laser on optimizing the onboarding process to guide each new user to the seven-friend milestone. According to Palihapitiya, Facebook reframed the entire onboarding experience, focusing hundreds of team members on this lone metric. As anyone can see with Facebook's meteoric user growth, the strategy worked exceptionally well.[1]

The key with the fulcrum and lever approach is to identify how you can double or triple your results with the same or less effort. It is not to simply improve results by five or 10 percent.

Achieving these types of outsized results takes questioning of the numbers. To identify ways to extend your lever for greater power, ask yourself:

- What would happen if you focused exclusively on a given metric?
- What would happen if you completely ignored that metric?

Then also ask yourself:

- What are all the upstream metrics that might play a more important role in the process?
- What are all the downstream metrics that might play a more important role in the process?

You of course should analyze all of your numbers and view your marketing data holistically. However, this exercise is helpful in forcing you to see the unique impact that different aspects of your marketing have. Not all metrics are created equal. Not all metrics will extend your lever. Find the ones that produce exceptionally large returns.

Double Down

Do not be afraid to change course in mid-stream when it comes to your marketing plan. If you identify a critical fulcrum that directly drives growth...double down on it!

I previously wrote about my experience at a digital marketing agency where a colleague and I redirected the company away from years of expensive industry conferences towards local, branded events. We initially tested a few local events in only one city (Chicago). When merely a few events produced multiple seven-figure contracts for the agency, we went all-in and the agency did a roadshow around the country. As mentioned, the local events immediately started bringing in seven figure accounts and became the number one lead driver for the company within 12 months. If we had dabbled, the opportunity would have been lost.

A similar all-in approach was taken by Dave Karraker, VP of Marketing and Communications at Campari America, the world's sixth-largest premium wine and spirits company. The

Campari brand has been around since 1860 and reached its peak in the U.S. market in the 1970's. Since then, sales had flattened out at 50K cases a year.

Campari marketing had traditionally focused on the educated, high-level cultural elite. A few years ago, attendance at two events that Campari participated in convinced Karraker it needed to change its focus. Immediately.

The first was a fashion event. Karraker and his team looked around the room and noticed nothing but "dead soldiers" – half drunk glasses of Campari cocktails. The next night they went to a foodie event and found the exact opposite. It was a younger crowd and there was nary a dead soldier in sight. It was an epiphany for Karraker.

He realized what he was seeing in the younger crowd was a changing pallet – one that thanks to Starbucks and the switch to foods like kale and brussels sprouts – had evolved to re-educate the American pallet to embrace more bitter tastes.

Karraker thought that if they liked bitter food then bitter cocktails could work, as well. Campari had a drink called Negroni – a super bitter drink that fit the bill. He immediately decided to forget the company's history and to focus on the art and fashion market, moving to embrace bitter.

He doubled down on his new focus, threw all the existing marketing out the window and went all-in on the bitter market. The brand targeted the Negroni marketing toward bartenders for two years. It ran bartender events and cocktail competitions. It jumped on social media to see which bartenders were talking about Negroni. It amplified those who were touting the Negroni brand by retweeting, reposting, and liking those bartenders to help reinforce their decision.

The pivot was a rousing success. In five years, Campari grew from 50K cases a year to over 100K.[2]

The message is clear. Do not be afraid to change course quickly when opportunity arises.

Too many marketers are afraid to pivot, and to do so boldly. Keep your eyes open for that "aha" moment when something begins to stand out. Look for that new metric (like the number of dead soldiers at an event in the case of Campari) that reveals the underlying Zeitgeist. That is when you need to double down and go all-in. Take it as far as you can and allow the growth to fund the additional effort.

Victory goes to the bold.

You Can Measure Anything

When marketers discuss metrics, they often focus on what is standard in their industry. Do not get hung up on these mainstream metrics. Determine what is important to growing your business by seeking the source influencing factors, and then find a way to measure them. An effective way to do that is to keep seeking the influencers of the influencers of the influencers in your marketing results.

For example, at Stratabeat, our agency, we measure revenue and profits, and we break the numbers down by client account every month, as well. We look at our leads, and the marketing initiatives and costs involved in lead generation. We also analyze our website activity, email analytics, and referral numbers. The source of all of these metrics, we have found, is our time.

We therefore track our time...down to the second.

No matter what we are doing, whether a new brand strategy for a client or even just processing vendor invoices, we track it. We use easy-to-use time tracking software on our laptops and on our phones, so that time tracking is as easy as a click of a button.

We know how much time is spent on each client account and specifically how the time was used, but we also know how much time is spent on non-client work such as administrative or marketing tasks for our own business. We then have analytics that helps us to understand immediately if any metrics are off, enabling us to explore the underlying reasons and to take corrective action quickly. As a result, we ensure that we are spending time on each client account in the right way, and that each individual at our agency is spending time aligned to priorities. Without such analytics, it would be guesswork to figure out whether our team is spending time optimized towards customer success as well as our own growth.

There are other unconventional metrics you can consider. For example, if thought leadership is your goal, you can measure elements of your activities that would clearly state if you are achieving success – number of engagements, media mentions, byline articles, interviews, social shares, downloads, awards, etc.

What are you hoping to gain from thought leadership? More leads? More orders? If so, you should be measuring those numbers directly resulting from your thought leadership campaigns, as well.

I have run into countless companies that have defined thought leadership as a goal, but have no metrics or tracking to determine their progress toward achieving it. At the end of the year, it is anyone's guess as to whether the efforts were sufficient, whether they were successful, or whether they were a failure. What typically happens is the marketing team points to *any* success in its efforts to claim success overall. This is just warped logic.

If you are looking to make more speaking appearances, for example, then by all means set a clear goal and track the number of events at which you speak. Taking it a step further, define the number of speaker applications you need to submit in order to hit your target number. Of course, out of all of these efforts, document the number of leads generated and compare them to the costs involved.

Finally, where is the scorecard for your metrics? Where are they tracked and how often is the scorecard reviewed? Is it easily accessible online? Who is ultimately responsible? Without accountability, protocols, and a calendar to ensure consistent implementation and management, your efforts will likely be too undefined and the data underutilized.

As explained in the *Rethink Your Goals* chapter, setting vague goals and winging it is a waste of time. Goals need to be clearly defined and supported by specific metrics, based on underlying documentation, reporting, and an analysis process.

Otherwise, you are just hoping. And as it has been stated before, hope is not a strategy.

Focusing On Results

One company I recently came across had been creating many blog posts each month. Unfortunately, the posts were boring, not worthy of being shared, contained grammatical errors, and were not optimized for organic search. In looking at the blog's analytics, not surprisingly, we found that the posts were not driving traffic and were delivering shockingly low page view numbers whether organically sourced or from visitors *already on the site!*

It goes without saying that the blog was not driving leads.

Why dedicate this much time to blogging if all you end up with are these types of dismal results? The company was focused on the number and frequency of blog posts it was producing each month, and expecting to magically get more views, visits, and leads. Going through the motions will not get you what you need. You have to expend the time and effort to make something incredible that is worth all the effort.

Do not focus on checking off boxes in a spreadsheet. Do not focus on metrics for the sake of metrics. Focus on measurements that will provide insights and guide you in taking actions that will improve your business results.

Marrying Goals With Metrics

As we have just discussed, metrics are not an end in themselves but are a means to an end. They need to be helping you understand what is happening in your business so that you can make changes that improve your marketing results. The way to ensure that is to align your metrics with your marketing goals.

Here is a case where being infatuated with an idea completely clouded a company to reality. The brand was captivated with the concept of inbound marketing. Great. However, its stated goal was to generate *immediate* leads.

As I worked through a marketing plan with the team, it was obvious they wanted results *now*, not in six months or even three months. They wanted leads piling up that week, the next week, and the week after that. They claimed it was an urgent situation and they needed to show their investors lead numbers ASAP.

I recommended a variety of tactics to drive leads immediately such as advertising, paid search, search remarketing, site retargeting, email marketing, and direct mail.

The team was having none of it. Due to their obsession with inbound marketing, they wanted "organic leads," not those paid by advertising or campaigns. Well, ok, that is fine, but inbound marketing takes time. When done well, it works great. But the results build slowly and compound over time. It is not something to do when you need instant leads, with investors breathing down your neck.

With paid media, we could have started a quick campaign in the morning and the brand would have begun seeing leads later in the day. That just is not the case with SEO, blogging, byline articles, social media, PR, video marketing, or other types of inbound marketing. Ugh.

Ultimately, our agency needed to separate ways with the company. The brand's lack of understanding of the need to marry marketing tactics with marketing goals was too large a schism. We walked away. Unsurprisingly, the brand's lead generation since that time has been a failure.

If you are going to drive results, you need to marry your metrics to your marketing goals, and this means marrying your tactics to the types of numbers you need to see in the time you need to see them. It just will not work if you do not. End of story.

Break Everything Down Into Numbers

For every marketing initiative, determine what you are measuring, and define the reason why.

At one point I was volunteering on an entrepreneurship council at a large university in the Boston area. The organization was in the process of a website redesign for the council when I joined its marketing steering committee. It was well on its way and had already developed the site taxonomy and initial wireframes.

Sounds great, right? Well, not so fast...

I asked the group to outline its goals and how they would be measured. Silence... Instead, they were all just busy redesigning the site. Not one person could speak to a specific goal of the redesign, or what the new site had to achieve differently than the current site. No numbers. No metrics. No key performance indicators.

The group was just looking to build a "better website". But when I asked them to define what a "better website" would be, and define it in a measurable way so that we could configure the associated tracking processes and assess performance, there was more silence.

The organization had multiple tiers of membership. I asked about the different goals associated with each tier of membership, as that, to me, would help us make better decisions as to what the new site would need to look like. After all, prioritizing gold-level membership at a much higher membership fee would require different strategies than prioritizing basic memberships. Again, silence.

Trying to make your website "better" is not going to get you what you want. You need a clear definition of your goals and specific success metrics to measure actual performance.

The Metrics That Matter To The C-Suite:

Remember that the metrics you focus on every day in your marketing may be different than the metrics you report to the C-Suite.

What matters to a marketer is typically the metrics that fill the marketing funnel. But when communicating to the C-Suite, you need to remember to leave the details behind and to focus on what moves the business. CEOs are numbers driven. But they have to be the right numbers.

Impressions? Forget about them.

Cost per click? In the trash can.

Revenue increased? Customer acquisition cost decreased? Net Promoter Score rose? Ah, that's better. Now we're talking.

Here is a sampling of the metrics the C-Suite is typically going to appreciate:

- Revenue
- Average Revenue Per Account
- Gross Profit
- Net Profit
- Return on Investment
- Number of Customers
- Number of New Customers
- Growth (Revenue Growth, Profit Growth, Customer Growth)
- Lifetime Value

- Customer Acquisition Cost
- Churn
- Net Promoter Score
- Etc.

When presenting to the C-Suite, make sure your metrics revolve around several key concepts – revenue, cost, and ROI. If you really want them to get excited, talk growth.

Learn to speak to the C-Suite in the following terms:

- **The Language of Levers** – Your executives want to know what the company can do to achieve greater growth more efficiently – with less effort or investment. What are the strategies you can recommend that would produce 2X, 3X, or 10X results?
- **The Language of Momentum** – It is always easier to grow when riding the waves of market change rather than fighting against any new market directions. What are the coming trends on which the brand should capitalize for an easier path to growth?
- **The Language of New Markets** – As mentioned previously, Bain & Company conducted a five-year study of growth-driving moves by 1,850 companies to determine how businesses achieve sustainable, profitable growth. The research revealed that companies realize their most ongoing, profitable growth when they push out the boundaries of their core business into an adjacent space. How can your data reveal new, related market opportunities that would be a natural extension from your core business today?
- **The Language of Segmentation** – How can you slice and dice the market further in order to dominate

specific audience segments? This might be geographic or demographic in nature. Or, it may be the difference in targeting a different department or title/role if B2B. Ownership of a segment is a very profitable proposition, and one that executives understand gives the brand a competitive edge.

- **The Language of Competition** – Whenever you educate your executive team on deeper insights into competitors' strategies, tactics, plans, and results, their ears perk up. They are always eager to understand the "Moneyball" of the market, where they can efficiently gain a competitive edge where a competitor is weak, using the wrong metrics, or simply not paying attention.

Dashboards

Does your marketing team use dashboards to measure performance? If not, work to change that immediately.

Would you ever think about driving a car without any indicators on the dashboard? You would never know how fast you were traveling, how much gas you had left in the tank, or how hot the engine was running. Totally ridiculous, right? So why would you run something much more valuable than your car – your marketing – without a view into your performance?

Dashboards provide a visual representation – a quick view – into the key performance indicators of your business. They deliver the following types of benefits:

- **Visibility** – You cannot manage what you do not know. With a quick glance, dashboards enable you to see what is going on in your marketing on a granular, below-the-surface level. With just a few minutes each day or week, you can keep your finger on the pulse of your marketing initiatives in a frictionless manner.

- **Early Detection** – If you rely on monthly or quarterly reports, it is quite possible that you will sometimes receive bad news late. Dashboards act as an early detection system, enabling you to spot red flags immediately and to take corrective action earlier.

- **Ongoing Improvements** – Dashboards allow you to measure your performance and take action to make needed improvements continually. Instead of making changes to your marketing based on your gut, you can base your decisions on real data and the trends revealed through your dashboards.

- **Common Language** – Dashboards provide you and your team a common language to quickly and easily understand performance. Regardless of whether you are the CMO or the Assistant Marketing Manager, dashboards accelerate communication and understanding among the entire team, providing clarity to your team members' purpose and actions.

- **Time Savings** – Data and information are growing by the day. Getting your hands on the right reports and consolidating them into actionable insight is time consuming. Dashboards take care of that by integrating a great deal of the relevant information you need in one place for quick review. You may need to dig deeper into your data than just the dashboards, but the dashboards point you to specific aspects of your marketing that require further attention, expediting the analysis process.

- **Performance Tracking and Mapping** – Many businesses with annual business plans are too often lacking indicators that map performance to the plan. Depending on the software in use, performance-to-plan metrics can be built into your dashboards to quickly show whether you are on track or whether you need to be taking corrective action based on your annual plan. This means that you can continually calibrate your marketing to increase the probability of achieving your annual goals rather than just relying on hope while your goals are filed away until the following year.

You can be throwing everything you have at the wall to see if it sticks, but if you do not have clear, visible metrics that you can see at the click of a mouse, you are at a severe disadvantage. Just like a car with no indicators, you are driving blind.

Dedicate Time To Analysis

How much time do you spend analyzing your marketing data? It is one thing to spend lots of time creating pretty reports. But if you are not spending most of your time on the analysis, it is a waste.

The value is in the analysis. Metrics are a good start, but they are only the starting line. Analysis is where you will figure out how to adjust, optimize, and unleash growth.

At the end of the day, your metrics are just more data. And we can all agree that we have plenty of data. But raw numbers, without context do not tell us anything. You need to get into the data, and understand what it means in the context of your business. That means digging into the root causes and determining ways to affect them.

You may know that your website visits are down. Or that your calls to action are not generating a sufficient number of clicks. You may be disappointed with the number of leads from your direct mail campaigns. Or, perhaps your customer surveys are returning feedback you never would have suspected.

Your metrics tell you the "what." Analysis reveals the "why," which is the first step toward "what do I do now."

Data analysis can help break down the big picture into smaller pieces that can be attacked one by one. It can help you glean valuable insights through trends and historical comparisons. Most importantly, it improves your decision making because it is based on real data, not anecdotes or emotion.

So, what percentage of your time is spent on analysis of your marketing data? What I have found is that many marketers do not have analysis time built into their schedules. This can lead to ad hoc analysis at random times, distorting the overarching conclusions being derived. It also can lead to cases where your memory becomes the driving force of your current actions. Instead, be sure to establish recurring analysis sessions in your calendar. These should by no means be the only times that you spend on analysis, but at the very least they provide you with an essential framework to ensure your data is being put to use consistently.

Moving beyond the metrics is how you will be able to develop theories and new ideas, uncover key insights, and establish relationships between disparate sets of data. Measuring is a critical start. But analyzing is the only true way to drive results.

Chapter Summary

Tom Malone, Professor of Management at MIT Sloan School of Management, stated, "If you don't keep score, you are only practicing." Metrics help you to not only play the game better, but to win the game. Marketing without metrics on the other hand results in randomness and a reliance on wishful thinking.

Yet even with established metrics, many marketing teams are focused on the wrong numbers. Too many brands blindly follow industry-standard metrics without thinking more deeply as to the alternatives that would move the needle more significantly. And some brands, even when they find the core metrics that make a significant difference, dawdle and lack the conviction to double down on the activities required to be successful. Some brands lack the convenient reporting dashboards to make the implementation more successful, or do not spend sufficient time on the analysis of the data to harvest the available insights to be gleaned.

Use data to your advantage by rethinking standard marketing metrics and blindsiding your competition in the process.

- What are your industry's standard marketing metrics?
- What are the marketing metrics on which your team currently focuses?
- Are you merely following the industry's norms, or have you dissected your marketing and uncovered alternative, underlying metrics that would move the needle more for your business?
- Is it possible that you need to revamp your branding in order for your metrics to have greater significance?
- Do you have metrics defined for the top, middle, and bottom of your funnel?
- What are the critical metrics on which your business needs to focus? Which metrics truly move the needle, and which ones are red herrings?

- How can you double down on your most important metrics to drive the biggest benefit?
- What can you eliminate in your marketing mix to re-allocate resources to focus on your key metrics?
- Do your metrics directly ladder up to your specific marketing goals?
- Have you created dashboards for fast, easy monitoring of your marketing performance?
- How much time do you dedicate to the analysis of your data? Are you missing out on key insights due to lack of analysis time?

6

RETHINK YOUR REVENUE MODEL

P roduct, Place, Price, and Promotion make up the traditional four "P's" of marketing. In many cases, price tends to become a primary focus of the marketing plan. More important than price, however, is the total revenue model – in other words, the methods, process, and framework by which your company makes its money.

Revenue is the top line of every P&L for a reason. Revenue is an enabler. It makes everything else possible. It empowers your organization to do more. By rethinking your revenue generation model, you can move beyond just paying your bills. You can invest, build, and dream big. You are able to introduce new products and services. You have the power to transform your business into your vision.

You can often achieve explosive business growth not necessarily by changing your product, but instead by changing your revenue model. How does your organization make money today? What is the current flow of revenue? How could you modify the model to achieve more revenue more reliably, even without any changes to your product or service itself?

Perhaps you currently charge your customers by product or service when instead you could move to a subscription-based pricing model. Salesforce.com pioneered this concept in the software industry with the introduction of its SaaS (Software as a Service) product in 1999, flipping the traditional software licensing model on its head with low monthly subscription fees. Salesforce went on to become the fastest enterprise software company to reach $6 billion in annual revenue.

Now that is rethinking the revenue model!

Aligning To Customers' Underlying Needs

When looking at your revenue generation, it is a good idea to start with your target audience. Too often, revenue models persist even after customer needs have evolved and would be better served otherwise.

Hilti, a Liechtenstein-based, high-end power tool manufacturer serving the construction industry, changed its revenue model to be better aligned with its customers' underlying needs. Founded in 1941, Hilti had long sold power tools directly to its customers. The company reviewed its existing model and reconsidered the value proposition for its customers.

Hilti noticed that contractors make money by *using* tools, not by *owning* them. So instead of selling equipment, it rethought its revenue model and began selling the *use* of the equipment instead, helping its customers to increase their productivity while reducing their capital investments. Hilti took over managing its customers' tool inventory, providing the right tool on demand and supplying tool repairs, replacements, and automatic upgrades for a monthly fee.

Hilti's innovative approach to charging for its tools solved a variety of problems with which the construction industry had been unsuccessfully grappling. Drilling tools require a large upfront investment. Broken machines during construction projects can cause major financial losses. Typically, repair services are not immediately available in the field. Uncertain reliability of tools causes many contractors to overstock to prevent emergency situations from arising in the case of tool failure.

After Hilti made the revenue model change, many contractors, who had spread their tool purchases among a number of manufacturers in the past, started allocating a greater share of purchases to Hilti in line with the benefits of the more holistic tool management service. Furthering the gains for Hilti, the new solutions model had higher margins than selling each product one by one, plus the ongoing service contracts led to longer and deeper customer relationships. This, in turn, provided Hilti with even greater insights into its customers' needs.[1]

Hilti rethought its revenue from a product-based model to a product-service-solutions-support model with great success, but it had to begin by examining its current revenue generation model and looking for ways to improve while adapting to a changing customer value proposition. When you rethink your own revenue model, you would be hard pressed to find a better place to start than with the underlying needs of your customers.

Entertaining A New Idea

In addition to exploring your customers' underlying needs, you can also uncover new revenue models through delivery methods that are more direct with customers. It is common to think that the way a product is delivered today is the only way it could possibly be delivered. Of course, that is myopic thinking and often blinds marketers to new possibilities.

For example, take the home entertainment market. The explosion of VHS tapes and players in the 1980's made in-home movie watching ubiquitous.

Blockbuster rode the wave by establishing a new routine for families – going to the video store to rent low-cost movies. Opening its first store in 1985, Blockbuster grew to 5,000 retail outlets and 60,000 employees. By 2002, Blockbuster's market cap had grown to $5 billion. Eight years later, it filed for bankruptcy. What happened?

Netflix.

Blockbuster was cemented in its brick and mortar business model and never anticipated the threat posed by the development of DVD technology. According to reports, the seeds of Blockbuster's demise were sown in 1997 when Reed Hastings, co-founder of Netflix, was upset at being charged a $40 late fee for failing to return the movie *Apollo 13* on time because he had misplaced the VHS cassette.

Hastings and co-founder Marc Randolph rethought the movie rental model and developed a more convenient method of obtaining movies to rent – while eliminating the hated late fees. Netflix offered flat rate DVD movie rentals by mail. The business originally started as a single rental service but in 1999 moved away from the per-rental model into a subscription-based model where customers paid a flat fee for unlimited rentals without due dates, late fees, or shipping and handling charges.

With the change in revenue model, annual sales rocketed from $1 million to $5 million within a year. Within five years, Netflix grew to $500 million and three years later hit $1 billion in revenue. In 2002, Netflix had one million subscribers,[2] and this grew to a whopping 93 million+ in 2016.[3]

Wisely, Netflix was determined not to suffer the same fate as Blockbuster and continued to rethink its model. It saw streaming as the big threat to its DVD mail order business and began a streaming service in 2011. It struggled deciding how to structure its business, first bundling with the DVD service and raising prices, then considered a separate business for streaming only, and then returned to a bundled service with options. Despite the fits and starts, Netflix continues to rethink its revenue model to stay viable in the marketplace. It has now moved into the realm of content creation by producing hit series like *House of Cards*, *Jessica Jones*, and *Orange is the New Black*.

Adam Hartung, author of the book *Create Marketplace Disruption: How to Stay Ahead of the Competition*, has long been bullish on Netflix mainly because the company leadership has consistently "shown a penchant for having the right strategy to remain a market leader – even when harshly criticized for taking fast action to deal with market shifts."[4]

Keeping Its Head In The Cloud

"You're an idiot. That's the stupidest thing. This is never going to work."

That was the reaction Salesforce.com CEO Marc Benioff got from his future co-founders when he unveiled his big idea in 1999. Benioff eventually convinced the three of them, and now Salesforce is an $8 billion powerhouse, the pioneer in the software-as-a-service (SaaS) business model.[5] Salesforce is yet another example of the power of a subscription-based revenue model.

Before getting any traction with the new model, though, Benioff had to take on an industry entrenched in enterprise software companies with expensive software that took years to implement. He turned the CRM market upside down by introducing a new business and technology model of delivering a cloud-based product to customers around the world for a monthly subscription fee. It was a classic rethinking of an existing model that resulted in a subscription service that was dirt-cheap and could be up and running the same day.

The new model was attractive when compared to the legacy, on-premises CRM software solutions from Oracle, SAP, Siebel Systems, and other enterprise vendors that were not only expensive to purchase, but required capital intensive hardware and a support team to manage.

Salesforce helps organizations manage interactions with prospects, leads, and customers, organizes sales pipelines, and enables slice-and-dice reporting on all sales activities. The real value is providing customers with a solution that eliminates the need for expensive IT infrastructure, dramatically reduces drawn out installation timelines, and easily integrates with other existing applications.

The new model not only eliminated the upfront capital expense, but also cumbersome and expensive multi-year licensing and professional service fees. Salesforce has now moved beyond CRM into online support and help desk, digital marketing, and analytics services.

It deploys a mixed-bundling revenue strategy where customers can choose from standalone versions of the software and bundled versions with performance features.

Salesforce continues to rethink its model by expanding from a SaaS model into a platform provider. Third party developers can now use the company's APIs to develop solutions on the Force.-com, Heroku, and Salesforce1 platforms. The platform option adds value for customers who need to fill product gaps while allowing Salesforce to capture revenue from platform licenses and listing fees from developers.[6]

The results have been phenomenally successful. As mentioned, Salesforce was the fastest enterprise software company to reach $6 billion in annual revenue. On top of this, the company is projecting revenue for fiscal year 2018 at more than $10 billion.[7]

Turns out it was not such a "stupid" idea after all.

The Razor-And-Blades Model

The razor-and-blades revenue model has become so popular that it defines an entire genre. When you are in a meeting and someone invokes "the razor-and-blades-model," most everyone knows immediately what that means. It is the idea of growing an installed base by offering a one-time product at little or no cost that requires repeated purchases of a complementary product. The vast majority of the revenue (if not all of the revenue) then comes from the complementary product.

For Gillette, the pioneer in shaving blades, that meant selling the razor handles at a low price – even as a loss leader – and then making up the profit on the subsequent purchase of razor blades.

Randall Picker, a professor at The University of Chicago Law

School, has done extensive research on Gillette's history with the model and notes that the company came up with the idea in 1921 following the expiration of the patents on the razor blade handle it had developed in 1904.

While the patents were in effect, Gillette sold its handles at a relatively high price – almost five times the competition. Once the patents no longer offered protection, Gillette lowered the cost of the handles to match the competition. It then raised the price of its blades by reducing the number of blades in a package from 12 to 10 but keeping the price the same. Gillette handle sales soared thanks to a deal with the U.S. government during World War I combined with the new low pricing on the formerly high-end handle. As a result, the company's user base – and profits – grew quickly.[8]

Getting To The Cutting Edge Of The Mail Order Business

The Gillette "razor-and-blades" model has been the standard for many years in such market and people have become accustomed to purchasing razors and razor blades in packs in their local stores. However, the competition is closing in by rethinking that model.

Dollar Shave Club has developed a new razor blade model. CEO Michael Dubin strived to solve what he felt was a basic problem for men: razor blades are really expensive when bought in the store. Getting there can be a hassle, and getting someone in the store to unlock the display can be frustrating.

Dubin created a membership service providing razors and blades by mail, launched a beta site, and began distribution out of his apartment. After a $100,000 round of angel funding, he relaunched in early 2012 and began using a fulfillment house. Dollar Shave Club did $4 million in revenue in 2012, $19 million in 2013, $65 million in 2014,[9] and $152 million in 2015.[10] It has captured more than 15 percent of the U.S. men's razor cartridge market and is serving more than 3 million people.[11]

Although the idea of a different revenue model was key to the success of the Dollar Shave Club, the company success began and was propelled by superb marketing. Durbin was able to get his Series A round of financing thanks to a clever video about the new business that had gone viral, as explained in the Rethink How They Think chapter.

Shaving equipment for men is an old, old business. It is not like the tablet computer or drone market. What Dollar Shave Club proved is that taking an old business and simply flipping the revenue generation model on its head can drive exceptional growth, even with essentially the same product as all others in the market.

In 2016, Unilever bought Dollar Shave Club for $1 billion. That is the benefit of rethinking your revenue model.

Portfolio Optimization

As evidenced by the above examples, ongoing, membership- or subscription-based revenue models have a great deal to offer. This, though, should not be thought of as limited to only one type of revenue stream.

Take our agency, Stratabeat. Although several of our services work on a retainer-based model, other services are project-based. We structure the pricing based on the nature of the work and what makes the most sense for clients.

Something like the development of a brand strategy, new logo, website design, or marketing collateral is project-based. Once a brand strategy is in place, after all, the client should not require a new one for a long time.

Lead generation, though, is retainer-based, covering services such as marketing consulting, SEO, PR, and conversion optimization. In addition, once a new website is launched, we charge for ongoing website maintenance on a retainer basis.

In this way, each client gets a custom mix of services, with the appropriate payment models. Everyone benefits from predictability, but sometimes you need to mix in one-off services as well in order to give the customer what they need in the optimal manner.

This type of portfolio optimization can be done across many industries. In our case, it is branding, design, and marketing services. This would be just as applicable in the case that you sold accounting services, though. Imagine a business that offers an annual budgeting service, or financial performance workshops, or a one-time audit service to ensure businesses are not wasting money and are using available cash effectively. Such business could also be offering ongoing, retainer-based accounting, budgeting, bookkeeping, and financial reporting services, as well as payroll and human resource administration.

So, explore mixing it up. If you run a business that sells each product or service as a one-off, brainstorm how to add ongoing offerings. If your model is currently subscription- or retainer-based, explore complementary individual products. A portfolio approach can be better aligned to your customers' needs, and it can strengthen your overall model by delivering both short-term and long-term revenue.

Cooking Up A New Model

The prior examples of revenue generation largely focus on one-time payment models compared to those that are ongoing in nature. The latter reduces risk for your business, but it is not the only method for reducing business risk in the revenue model.

Take the restaurant industry as an example. The typical restaurant includes a lot of unpredictability such as last-minute cancellations and food spoilage. Yuck!

The restaurant business does not normally lend itself to innovation, but chef Grant Achatz and business partner Nick Kokonas wanted to eliminate the vagaries of the traditional reservation-based, standard menu model. In 2011, they conceived an entirely new idea – restaurant as theater called Next Restaurant. Located in Chicago, Next sells season tickets for its "productions" that change three times a year. Diners purchase tickets upfront – sometimes costing as much as $125 (not including drinks). Its themed menus have included "Paris 1906," "Childhood," and "Thailand," as well as "The Hunt," "South America," and "French Cuisine from Napa Valley."

Next has accumulated an impressive array of awards, including a James Beard Foundation Award for Best New Restaurant, AAA Four Diamond Award, multiple Jean Banchet Awards, and an unprecedented 12 four-star reviews from the Chicago Tribune, according to the restaurant's website. Elite Traveler included the restaurant in its list of the Top 100 Restaurants in the World.

The beauty of the model is that once a ticket is sold, it cannot be cancelled – eliminating the costly no-show expense that can ruin a restaurant's bottom line. Business has been brisk, with upwards of 20,000 people sometimes clamoring for tickets. Just like with sporting events and concerts, a robust secondary market has opened up for people looking to get tickets.

Achatz and Kokonas keep their financials close to the vest, but based on the diner response, it is safe to say that the new model is a delicious success.

Falling Far From The Tree

Up to now, the examples in this chapter have focused on the direct correlation between products/services and the revenue your business charges for them. Going beyond this concept, you can increase revenue even more by creating an ecosystem underlying, supporting, and fueling your revenue generation. An ecosystem empowers your business to grow exponentially rather than incrementally.

A good example of this is Apple.

How many people love their PCs? Or their Windows operating system? Not many. And even though 80 to 90 percent of computer users are on PCs, there is not any real affection there. Users basically tolerate their PCs.

But Apple? That is another story. Even though Mac users make up only a small fraction of computer users, they are raving fans devoted to their Mac OS in cult-like fashion. They view Mac as being of higher quality, with better security, and exponentially better customer service. (Ever visit an Apple Store?)

But here is the thing. Apple is not just a computer manufacturer. That may be its legacy, but it has been able to rethink its revenue model and transformed from a hardware company selling computers (and even printers at one point) into an entire ecosystem with platforms like iTunes, iCloud, and App Store while changing the way we communicate with the revolutionary iPhone. Even the iPhone itself is an ecosystem of apps.

How was Apple able to transcend the hardware world to become an integral part of everyone's lives?

It should come as no surprise that Steve Jobs, the charismatic co-founder and famous "rethinker," stands at the middle of the evolution of Apple. Jobs and co-founder Steve Wozniak looked at things differently right from the inception of the company in the 1970's, when they viewed computers not as tools for the technorati but as devices that could improve personal efficiency. With that mindset, the first Apple computers were designed with the user in mind.

By the mid 80's however, the Mac was only a niche product as the IBM/Microsoft behemoth set the standard for personal computer use and dominated the market. In 1985, Apple dismissed Jobs and for the next 12 years drifted under the guidance of three different CEO's, each dabbling in a different strategy. There was no coherent plan of action and many experts predicted the end was near for Apple.

Jobs was brought back to the company in 1997 and began the transformation. He reduced the number of Apple products from 15 to four. Then the turnaround began. He created the iPod, which led to the iTunes platform and the beginning of the shift from computer manufacturer to ecosystem builder. He made peace with Bill Gates and began a partnership with Microsoft to keep Apple viable in the personal computer marketplace.

However, that was only the beginning. Jobs was rethinking Apple and had a bigger plan.

What followed in the first decade of the 21st century was a parade of products built on Jobs' platform strategy: iMac, iPod, iPhone, Apple TV, and the iPad. The goal was to attract customers to the world of Apple, an interconnected universe of gadgets that fulfilled users' computing, entertainment, and communications needs. The iPod and then iPhone increased in value with the more music and videos purchased in the iTunes store. The iTunes store became more critical to Apple users who wanted to increase the value of their iPods and iPhones. We have not even touched upon the world of accessories to support Apple's ecosystem of platforms and products, but these of course contributed more revenue to the mix.

The results of rethinking the Apple revenue model and introducing the Apple ecosystem have been stunning. Revenue grew from $7.1 billion in 1997 to more than $215 billion in 2016.[12] Apple is now one of the most valuable companies on the planet.

All because Jobs rethought the company's business and revenue model in the form of great products within a great ecosystem.

Finally Making The Grade

Sometimes you have to rethink your model more than once to get the right results. That was the case for Payal Kadakia, Co-Founder and Executive Chairman of ClassPass – a popular monthly membership service that provides subscribers with access to a variety of fitness and dance classes. The monthly fee allows subscribers to sign up for an unlimited number of classes in pilates, boxing, spinning, aerial yoga, and many others.

Kadakia, an avid dancer who was born in India, moved to New Jersey as a child and studied economics and operations research at MIT, founded the company in 2010. She came up with the idea when she struggled searching for dance classes she wanted to take. She just could not get enough information and recognized an opportunity for a business.

However, it took a couple of false starts to get the model just right. Her first effort, Classivity, received tons of page views, but not many bookings – a major problem since her revenue model was based on the number of people who actually booked a class.

Two years later she tweaked the model and launched Passport. This service gave users 10 chances to try one class at a new studio. Scammers figured out a way to continue to return to their favorite classes by using fake emails and that ultimately tanked that idea.

Kadakia and her Co-Founder Sanjiv Sanhavi brought on marketing veteran Mary Biggins who had been with fintech startup Betterment and also VistaPrint to help scale the next generation of the service. The third time was the charm.

Now renamed ClassPass, the new model launched in 2013 offered customers an unlimited number of classes for $99 a month – with only three classes allowed in the same studio in any given month. That was the magic model, catching on quickly, with 350,000 classes booked in the first three months.[13] This success allowed Kadakia to expand the company into other cities.

ClassPass raised $84 million to fund the growth and today the service is available in cities across four countries with estimated sales of $60 million.[14] Kadakia and her team continue to rethink ClassPass's model, offering various other subscription plans tailored to local needs. The company's long term vision includes incorporating other experiences like cooking and massages.

ClassPass is now valued at nearly $400 million[15] and Forbes estimates Kadakia's net worth at almost $50 million.[16] Subscriber growth doubled from 2015 to 2016, and the company reports that Q1 of 2107 is to be the highest growth quarter ever for the company.[17]

If at first you do not succeed...

From Web Design To SEO To SaaS

Sometimes, you need to rethink not only your revenue model, but also the actual business itself – what it is that you are selling. The story of Moz is an example of how organizational leaders should continually search for the right revenue-generation model, and may need to pivot the business in order to identify a model that is sustainably profitable.

I earlier wrote about Rand Fishkin, the founder of Moz. Fishkin began as a web designer in the early 2000's. He learned that the success of the sites he designed depended on how high they ranked in search engine results pages (SERP). He dove into the world of search engine optimization (SEO) to help his clients get the highest possible rankings. His first move was to use outside contractors to find the best possible SEO techniques.

As demand for SEO resources grew, so did the cost, and Fishkin decided to develop the expertise in-house. Through relentless research and investigation, Fishkin eventually became an SEO expert and began his SEOmoz blog in 2004.

The SEO business quickly attracted a following, but there was one problem: his company was not making any money. As the blog began generating a steady stream of readers, Fishkin expanded the business to include SEO consulting. It was then that Fishkin hit on the model that would lead to a significant revenue stream: paid subscription software.

In 2007, Fishkin began selling the digital tools Moz was using in-house via a SaaS model. By 2009, Moz was a full-time software publisher, selling three products – Moz Pro for SEO professionals featuring tools like Keyword Explorer and Open Site explorer, Moz Local aimed at helping local businesses with their profiles, and Moz API, for individuals who wanted direct access to the raw data.

Fishkin informed me that the evolution into a software business was mostly accidental. "We launched our tools as a subscription on somewhat of a whim, simply wanting to share them with others but not being able to handle the volume of totally free access," he explained. "Within a few months, it was clear that we had a potentially exciting, real business, and we began investing in it more seriously."

In the fall of 2007, Moz received $1.1 million in venture capital and by September of 2010 it was ranked #334 on the Inc. 500 list of fastest growing companies. Another round of funding in May 2012 brought $18 million into the business, allowing the company to expand to over 150 employees. Today the Moz site gets almost three million visitors a month.[18] Its customer base continues to grow with roughly 36,000 users and $42.6 million in revenue in 2016.[19]

The self-effacing Fishkin remains humble about his company's dramatic growth. "I think we got so lucky mostly because we'd already built out a great marketing channel for customer acquisition over many years prior – the Moz blog," he says. "That's something I'd encourage a lot of other entrepreneurs to consider – how you can potentially build an audience for your product before you launch it."

But do not let Fishkin's modesty fool you. It was not luck. It was his ability and willingness to rethink his revenue model that allowed Moz to prosper.

Freemium

On the topic of SaaS software, the industry provides a good example of the freemium model as an option for revenue generation. In the freemium model, the base product is offered free of charge, with premium options available for a fee. The freemium model overcomes the potential roadblock of offering a 30-day free trial or other limited offer, in that ongoing services are of greater appeal and make the probability of a conversion much greater.

Examples of this revenue model include uber-successful businesses such as Slack, LinkedIn, Box, Dropbox, Evernote, Canva, Hulu, MailChimp, and HootSuite.

One of the keys to a freemium model is investing fully in reaching a critical mass of users. In the case that your product is valuable, the idea is to get people hooked on it, so that they cannot imagine *not* being able to use it. The second part of the equation is that the premium services need to be enough of a value-add to a sufficient percentage of users that such users convert to being paying customers. It is of little use to have huge numbers of customers if none of them are paying a dime.

Keep in mind that with freemium products, it is critical that the offering is straightforward and immediately understandable, as is the value proposition. Also, equally important is that the incremental cost of onboarding a new user needs to be negligible, or the model will collapse under its own weight.

The idea of offering a free base product and charging for only premium features or services is an effective means for acquiring a large customer base, but only businesses with operating costs aligned to supporting huge numbers of non-paying users should consider this as a viable option.

Although the freemium model is popular with SaaS products, it is certainly not limited to software. Consider the music group Smashing Pumpkins. It released an album that could be downloaded without cost, and instead made money from related merchandise and ticket sales. Whether your business is software or music, or consulting or education, with creativity there are ways to structure a base product for free while charging for premium additions.

Tripling Revenue Through A New Pricing Model

Rethinking your revenue model should also mean applying the Pareto Principle, better known as the 80/20 rule, to whatever current model is in place to extract more value from your existing customer base. As with the freemium model, sometimes the vast majority of your revenue is going to come from a small percentage of your customers. One of the keys to rethinking your revenue is to figure out how to create more value out of the 80 percent of your customers (or whatever percentage is applicable to your own brand) who are providing merely 20 percent or less of your revenue today.

That 80 percent may be a deep resource of untapped, additional revenue, yet too many companies ignore this potential and allow the 80 percent to continue in the same low-value mode as they always have. This creates a significant drag on your business overall, limiting your growth.

An example of a company that effectively attacked the 80 percent of clients representing the smallest amount of revenue is

Snipcart, a SaaS ecommerce solution for developers. Snipcart found a way to not only make the 80 percent more profitable, but also eliminate any clients not willing to pay their fair share.

In the process, Snipcart *tripled* its revenue.

Snipcart was launched in 2013 by a self-described team of "hard-core geeks and developers" to offer developers a flexible, HTML/JS based shopping cart solution. The founders recognized that there were plenty of e-commerce solutions around for merchants, but almost none for web designers and developers, who were the ones actually building the solutions. They created Snipcart to make it easy to add ecommerce to any website.

Wanting to grow its business quickly, Snipcart offered an aggressive pricing model to attract clients – 2 percent of sales generated. Its straightforward tagline was, "If you sell, we get paid. If you don't, we don't."

The model worked as hoped and Snipcart built a customer base of nearly 2,000. After two years, it did some analysis of its customer activity and found that, in line with the Pareto Principle, 80 percent of its revenue was coming from 20 percent of its customers. Unfortunately, approximately eight out of 10 customers were using the platform virtually free. Worse yet, those were the customers that were swamping Snipcart's support organization.

Snipcart's project manager suggested a solution: institute a flat minimum fee.

The founders were adamantly opposed, feeling that charging a minimum was a betrayal of the customers who had signed up based on the "if you don't get paid, we don't get paid" promise. However, after much gnashing of teeth and finally realizing the company could not continue to provide world-class support for customers who were not generating much revenue, they decided to move forward.

Snipcart settled on a flat minimum fee of $10 per month. Its analysis showed 80 percent of customers were generating less than $500 a month in revenue for their businesses. In effect, it would be asking the 80 percent to pay their fair share with no affect to its best customers, the 20 percent who were selling more than $500.[20]

The results were dramatic (and a little traumatic, as well).

Many were angry at the change in pricing model and threatened to stop using Snipcart. But the Armageddon some at the company were fearing never materialized. There was a slight two-to-three percent drop in signups, and the company lost half its customer base – all non-paying customers that did not impact revenue but eased the burden on support substantially. As expected, Snipcart did not lose one paying customer.

The impact on revenue was significant. New users signed on fully aware of the $10 flat fee and for those sub-$500 customers that stayed on, Snipcart instantly realized $10 each in added revenue. The result was a tripling of revenue that allowed the company to hire a new developer, accelerate product development, and improve customer support.[21] The company now boasts more than 5,000 customers[22], and each one contributing to Snipcart's bottom line.

Do Not Be Shy About Pricing

The key lesson from Snipcart is that you should ensure your business is getting value out of *all* of your customers, even the ones that fall into the "80" of the 80/20 rule. Part of that process is to rethink and test your pricing. You want to ensure your prices are high enough to maximize revenue. Underpricing is a more common problem than you may think, and is often a significant inhibitor of growth.

A vivid example of underpricing involved the Concorde in the 1980's. The Concorde, the world's first supersonic transport, was the only commercial aircraft capable of flying at twice the speed of sound.

British Airlines (BA) proudly ran a Concorde service for six years with only one, not insignificant problem. The routes were losing money. Lots of it. In 1982, the head of BA at the time, Sir John King, created a special Concorde division and turned it over to Captain Brian Walpole with one directive: turn the losses into profits in two years or we are shutting down Concorde operations permanently.

BA surveyed businesspeople on what they thought the price of a Concorde ticket should be. Most of them had no idea since most of them had secretaries or travel departments that booked all their arrangements. But when they were asked to guess, they all estimated the fare to be higher than it actually was.

BA immediately revised its pricing policy – upward – since there was obviously a gap in the perceived value of the service and what BA was charging for it. It doubled the price of a one-way ticket on the Concorde to what would be an astounding $7,000 today. The new pricing repositioned the Concorde as a luxury item for super-elite travelers and the rich and famous. Sales never suffered despite the massive increase, and the Concorde division quickly became profitable, making almost 500 million pounds (approximately $607 million, depending on the exchange rate).[23]

The message: chances are you are undervaluing your offering.

Your price should not be based on cost plus margin. It is about perceived value in the marketplace. Do not be afraid to find out what your product or service is worth.

One important reason for not undervaluing your product is that if you do, your potential customers will do the same thing. There is still a mindset with buyers that price equals value. Many assume a low-priced product must necessarily be of low quality, when in reality that is not the case.

A developer of consumer-oriented productivity software (who wanted to remain anonymous) was pleasantly surprised to discover this common misconception. He launched his product with a price point of $9.99. He was able to obtain a good amount of publicity on his launch from the tech media and started getting 50,000 daily visits to his website. Although traffic was robust, sales were not. Not many visitors were buying the product.

The budding entrepreneur redesigned his website but nothing changed: high traffic, low sales. Three months later, in an effort to generate some revenue from those few customers who were actually buying, he doubled the price to $19.99. Then the magic happened. Sales of the product spiked almost immediately – by a factor of 10!

He checked to see if he was getting additional press but there was nothing new. Traffic remained the same but the conversion rate had increased by 10X! Customers simply assumed a higher price meant a better product, and the developer reaped the rewards.[24]

That is a good example of the power of price to determine customer perception of value.

As mentioned earlier, social psychologist Robert Cialdini,

author of *Influence: The Psychology of Persuasion*, says the reason behind this phenomenon is that in "markets in which people are not completely sure of how to assess quality, they use price as a stand-in for quality."[25]

While most customers would not pay $25 or $50 for pencils, dental floss, or a comb because it is easy to compare them to other products, it is much harder to evaluate certain categories of products or services. Art, business consulting, and company valuation services, for example, all fall into that category. If you price your services very high, the prospect typically will default to thinking that your services are extremely high quality and better than the competition.

Rethink your pricing and make sure you are not sabotaging your own sales with pricing that is too low.

Pricing Power

As the Snipcart, Concorde, and productivity software stories illustrate, pricing changes can have a major impact on your revenue and must be thought through carefully.

According to McKinsey & Company, "pricing right is the fastest and most effective way for managers to increase profits."[26] The firm offers the example of an average income statement of an S&P 1500 company. Increasing the price one percent can generate an eight percent increase in operating profits, even if volumes do not change — an impact nearly 50 percent greater than reducing variable costs such as materials and direct labor and more than three times greater than the impact of a one percent increase in volume.

So, how do you go about changing your pricing to increase revenue?

Price Anchoring

One way to increase your prices is to leverage a cognitive bias that arises from anchoring, whereby people tend to rely on the first piece of information they receive to assess value in context.

In one study, people were asked to estimate the worth of a home. They were given pamphlets comparing the prices of homes in the surrounding neighborhood. Some were given actual prices and some were presented with prices that were intentionally overinflated. Those who had been given the artificially inflated prices had markedly higher estimates of the target home.[27]

Price anchoring can also be used as a basis of comparison for your prospective buyers, even when they encounter the pricing options all at the same time. When I worked at Panasonic in Japan, the company released many products. Whenever a new product was released, a premium, higher-priced version of the product was also introduced right alongside the product. That way, when people would consider the product, they would automatically feel that the lower-priced item was inexpensive and that they would be "saving money" with their purchase. This drove increased sales of the lower-priced item. In reality, the company had no intention of selling the higher-priced products, and used them simply as a price anchoring mechanism. Placing premium products and services near standard offerings creates a very strong value perception for customers.

For one of our agency's clients with three pricing tiers, we suggested that the client increase the price of each tier. People tend to purchase the middle-cost product when confronted with low-cost, middle-cost, and high-cost options. Sure enough, the middle product had been the most popular. After shifting all prices higher, customers still leaned towards the middle product option but were paying more than previously, and surprisingly, even the high-cost product sold out.

Keep Prices Short and Simple

When you display your prices, keep them as short as possible. A paper in the *Journal of Consumer Psychology* found that prices containing more syllables were perceived as higher to consumers, even when they were actually the exact same price.[28] When given the following three choices, the top two were perceived as much higher than the third:

- $1,499.00
- $1,499
- $1499

"One thousand four hundred and ninety-nine" vs. "fourteen ninety-nine" made the difference, even if the numbers were not said out loud.

Price Reframing

When displaying your price, consider the most palatable way to package it to your prospective customers. For example, if you sell a SaaS product with an annual cost of $1,200, you may choose to instead communicate the price as $100 per month. Or, you could explain that it is less than the daily cost of a cup of Starbucks coffee.

If you sell management consulting services, calculate the incremental revenue you could potentially deliver for your clients, and then compare that number to the cost of your services. All of a sudden, your six-figure price tag is a bargain compared to the impact to the business you would be delivering.

Of course, if you sell a luxury item, displaying the higher price may be the more effective strategy. The restaurant Fleur de Lys sells a $5,000 burger. A Ferrari GTC4Lusso will run you $300,000. It would be downright counterproductive to try to make either of these sound any less expensive. The crazy high pricing actually makes them even more attractive and desirable.

Framing your price effectively helps to spur more sales, but you need to customize this for your particular offering and audience. There is no cookie cutter solution.

Cross Sell to the Same Audience

Selling more to existing customers is far more efficient than acquiring brand new customers. If you already have a customer base that is happy with your products or services, explore ways to keep adding value to this group.

Noah Kagan is the founder of Sumo Group, with a suite of complementary offerings for digital marketers. KingSumo helps them sell more through online giveaways. His Sumo product suite helps them increase website traffic and acquire more customers. His AppSumo product introduces them to other marketing software products they may find useful at deep discounts. Once you are interested in one product, it is very easy for Sumo Group to attract you to its other related products, as the target audience is consistent across the board.

If you have multiple products or services, you can bundle them together to create attractive packages that are more efficient for your customers than purchasing and making use of each one individually. Or, build a tiered, sequential model for the consumption of your products/services, so that customers essentially graduate from one to the next to the next. Or, be a consultant to your customers beyond your products or scope of work, and treat the effort as an investment in market research; uncover new products and services you *should be* offering them to tackle those yet unresolved frustrations and pain points.

There are various methods for selling more to the same audience. Be creative and add as much incremental value as possible.

Chapter Summary

Your revenue is your lifeblood. With greater revenue, your business is stronger and your options for further growth multiply. With more revenue, you can spend more on innovation, marketing, and adding value for your customers.

Without revenue, your brand suffers. Without revenue, your brand is weak and vulnerable, and your options become limited.

Make a concerted effort to review the way your business generates revenue. Whether moving to a subscription model, or requiring upfront payment, or raising prices, or any of a number of other revenue strategies as outlined in this chapter, you can positively affect big change by attacking the revenue model head-on instead of adjusting the product, or service, or operations. As the stories in this chapter illustrate, making bold changes in your revenue model can often result in dramatic business growth.

Time to start rethinking how you make money.

- How does your business generate revenue today?
- How can you adjust your revenue model to make it more predictable?
- Is there any part of your business that could move to a subscription model to ensure an ongoing revenue stream?

- Can you offer an initial product at an affordable price to get your customers hooked, and then employ the razor-and-blades model to increase your customer lifetime value?
- How can you adjust your revenue model to secure a higher percentage of the revenue upfront, or earlier in the process?
- Can you build an ecosystem of products and services, offering your customers greater value and offering your business greater scalability?
- How can you eliminate customers that are a drag on the business?
- Or alternatively, how can your lowest revenue-generating customers (the 80 percent representing 20 percent of your revenue) contribute more to your bottom line?
- Is it time to raise your prices?
- Have you tested variations of the display of your pricing?
- How can you cross-sell to your existing customers in a way that adds significant value to their purchases?

7

RETHINK YOUR FUTURE

A t this point, you have taken the time to rethink six aspects of your marketing. You have analyzed your audience segmentation and understand how your audience members think. You have reframed your marketing goals, discovered new ways to reach your prospective customers to spark growth, and decided on your key metrics. In addition, you have reevaluated your revenue generation model to ensure an overarching structure specifically designed to maximize growth.

What does your future hold?

Now is the time to think about anticipation, innovation, and expansion. What is the "next big thing" in your industry? What waves of market momentum can you ride? What other ways can your business meet customer needs?

Wipro started out selling vegetable oil. It now provides global information technology, consulting, and outsourcing services and is known as the "IBM of India." It has grown annual revenue to $7.7 billion.[1] It's hard to believe that Wipro actually stands for Western India Palm Refined Oils!

To grow continually, what you sell today is not necessarily what you will sell in the future. The experience of other companies has shown that failure to consider your future can have devastating consequences. Consider the Fortune 500. Since 2000, more than half of the companies in the Fortune 500 have gone belly-up, been acquired, or shut down operations.[2] Yikes!

Remember the Fortune 500 company Republic Aviation? How about Cudahy Packing Company? Yeah, I didn't think so...

Fail to rethink, and be prepared to fail to survive.

Research in Motion (RIM) helped reinvent the concept of communication with its pioneering Blackberry smartphone. Its arrival on the scene in the late 1990's nearly singlehandedly tanked the pager business enabling people to send messages instead of pings or vibrations. Introducing the Blackberry in 1998, RIM quickly came to dominate the phone market, passing 1 million subscribers by 2004. By 2007, it had over 12 million subscribers and owned 60 percent of the market.

That was its peak as Apple launched the iPhone in 2007 and by 2012 had more than three times as many users as the Blackberry. RIM never rethought its future, failing to counter the Apple threat and ignoring the fact that people wanted mini-computers in their hands and not just phones. RIM has since fallen to less than one percent of the market. In 2016 it got out of the hardware business to focus on software only, but it is probably too late to save the company.

When you rethink your future, consider how you can revamp your core offering, or offer something completely new. It can often take just as much energy to do something with a small market potential as it does to create something with massive possibilities. Think big, and chances are your future growth will match. As Henry Ford once said, "Whether you think you can, or you think you can't – you're right."

We call that rethinking your future.

The 250-Year Plan

Regardless of the size or condition of your company, you can always plan for the future. If you feel your business is stagnant or stuck, consider the humble beginnings of corporate power-house Panasonic and its dynamic founder Konosuke Matsushita.

Matsushita, born in 1894, became an apprentice in a bicycle shop in Osaka at age nine to help his family survive. His father was a farmer who had gambled away the family's home and savings in bad investments. When Matshushita was 15 he left the bike shop, even though in those days it was unheard of for an employee to leave his first employer. He was captivated by the invention of electricity and wanted to make that a part of his life.

He became a wiring assistant at the Osaka Electric Light Company and then advanced to the role of inspector. At 20 he attended night school. He yearned for more and pitched the idea of light sockets to his boss, who was not interested in the idea.

His father had always taught him that success lay in being an entrepreneur, and Matsushita took that advice to heart by step-ping out on his own in 1917 at the age of 23 to establish his own company.

He set up shop in a tiny, dirt-floored tenement with only his wife and her 15 year-old brother as employees. Matsushita's savings at the time totaled less than 100 yen (roughly $1 dollar in today's terms), so power tools and equipment were out of reach. They would have to do things manually. They began producing Matsushita's light sockets, but sales were so poor that the company was on the brink of bankruptcy by the end of the first year. The company was saved thanks to an order for a thousand insulator blades for electric fans.

With the influx of revenue, Matsushita rented a two-story home and established Matsushita Electric Housewares Manufacturing Works, the forerunner of what would become the Panasonic Corporation. He then began tinkering at night with electrical designs, and introduced an attachment plug and a two-way electrical socket. As they were of higher quality and much cheaper than what was on the market at the time, sales were robust. By the end of 1918, he was employing 20 people. By 1922, he had to build a new factory to meet the demand for his products.

In 1923, Matsushita entered what he viewed to be a potentially lucrative market – the bicycle light business. Back then, it was common for cyclists to use candle and oil lamps on their bicycles. The battery-powered lamps available at the time were unreliable, often lasting only three hours.

Matsushita spent six months designing a bullet-shaped bike lamp that would operate for nearly 40 hours without a charge. However, the reputation for battery lamps was so bad at the time that wholesalers refused to market it.

Matsushita bypassed the wholesalers and went directly to bicycle shop owners, asking them to test the product themselves and offering to sell them on consignment – paying only for what consumers bought. Sales took off.

In 1927, Matsushita developed a second generation of the lamp and rebranded it as National. He then, because why not, moved the company into electro thermal products with the goal of producing affordable products with mass-market appeal. Three months later, he introduced the National "Super-Iron."

Appliances like clothes irons that produced heat electrically were financially out of reach of most households at the time. Matsushita bet on the market, ordered 10,000 units a month to be produced, and lowered costs dramatically. This allowed him to sell the iron 30 percent less than the competition and the Super-Iron became another bestseller. After the iron came an electric foot warmer at half the price of what others were charging.

Japan's national broadcasting station began transmissions in 1925, but radios at the time were expensive and unreliable. In 1930 Matsushita decided to jump into the radio business, developing the first three-tube radio, the R-31. To ensure development rights and to spur demand for the entire industry, Matsushita bought a critical patent to radio development and then proceeded to license it without cost to the rest of the manufacturers in the industry.

By 1932, the business was producing more than 200 different products. When it came to rethinking his company's future, Matsushita did not fool around. His company certainly took a different approach than RIM. At the commemoration of the company founding in 1932, Matsushita announced the company's long-term mission, which read in part, "to create material abundance by providing goods as plentiful and inexpensive as tap water." He then unveiled a 250-year plan for the company to fulfill that mission. The plan consisted of ten 25-year periods, each divided into three phases.[3] Now *that* is rethinking your future!

The following year the company started developing electric motors. In 1935 the number of products overall increased to 600, and an electric fan was unveiled as the first motor-run household product in 1936. The 1950s brought washing machines and TVs.

Today, Panasonic sells everything from audio and visual systems to shaving gear, from cameras and camcorders to power tools and ventilation equipment, from polymer capacitors to semiconductors, and from solar panels to streamlined IP communications equipment. Annual sales for the company now exceed $7 billion. Not too shabby for a company that started making fan insulator plates by hand on a dirt floor.

It is one thing to grow. It is another thing to continually reinvent your business to ensure you thrive over multiple decades. Panasonic is an example of seeing where the waves of the future are leading society, and being proactive to stay ahead of the game.

You may not be ready for a 250-year plan, but do you know where you need to be in three or five years? The future is coming whether you like it or not. Are you being proactive? Is your business ready?

Reimagining Your Brand's Future

What your company is today is not necessarily what it should be tomorrow. You may sell fan insulator plates today, but that does not mean you should not sell semiconductors in the future. Apple started out by selling computer boards. It now sells phones, tablets, data storage, apps, and music, not to mention computers, in a tightly integrated ecosystem.

Change is a constant in the business world. For many companies, failing to adapt to the constant change leads to bankruptcy or being acquired at a massive discount. RIM is a perfect example of a company that refused to adapt to the waves of change, and provides a stark contrast to both the approach and success of Apple.

As a marketing leader, you need to read the market, understand your audience, and see the change that is coming. You need to be working on two businesses – what you are doing today, and what you should be doing in the future to not only survive, but to thrive and grow. With this in mind, innovation and evolution are business imperatives. They need to be part of your company DNA if you hope to succeed in the future.

Recall the stories of many of the companies covered in this book, and you will see a common thread. Moz and Basecamp, for example, were web design companies that could have continued to grow those businesses. Instead, while servicing current customers, they had the vision to see new opportunities for their business and became fast-growing software publishers.

As previously explained, Moz founder Rand Fishkin saw the need for search engine optimization and so evolved Moz into a software developer, creating SEO tools for businesses and individuals. Today, Moz has 36,000 customers and revenue of more than $42 million.

Similarly, Basecamp was a website design agency, but founder Jason Fried saw something more in his company. He realized the project management tools his team had developed and was using internally could provide a lucrative product to drive his company into the future. Basecamp software user volume is now more than 15 million with over 100,000 companies as paying customers.

Reflect on the story of Marlin Steel Wire Products, "the king of the bagel baskets," who could have continued its march into oblivion by maintaining its existing business model. Instead, Drew Greenblatt bought Marlin, realized the bagel basket business was a dead end and reimagined the company's future. He targeted aerospace, chemical, defense, medical, and automotive businesses, met the more stringent demands of those industries, and grew annual revenue by roughly 10X.

Consider how Fitbit was able to see the threats around them from industry giants like Apple and Samsung and added a corporate wellness platform targeting large company health and fitness programs. This innovative shift is less competitive and has the potential to contribute to Fitbit's growth for years to come.

Think about how Netflix, the key disrupter of the video home rental business, anticipated the shift from physical media to online streaming. Netflix saw the future and dove into the world of streaming. It then took the business to another level by getting into content production to ensure it stayed ahead of its competition. Netflix now boasts more than 93 million users and over $8.8 billion in annual revenue, representing revenue growth of approximately 101.9 percent over the past three years.

These dynamic and visionary companies realized their markets would be changing. You need to understand that yours will, as well. Your customers' behavior is going to change. Your industry is going to change. The question is not *IF* you are going to change but *HOW* are you going to adapt to thrive in the future.

Going For The Moon

In the *Rethink Your Goals* chapter, I talked about President Kennedy's bold goal of reaching the moon by the end of the sixties. The proclamation served as a catalyst for a wave of technological advances that propelled the country from the laid back 50's into the energetic 60's and beyond.

It is appropriate then, that Larry Page, Co-Founder of Google, calls his outrageously ambitious projects "moonshots." Page founded Google with Sergey Brin in 1998 with the goal of organizing the seemingly infinite amount of information on the web. Within a month Google had 10,000 searches a day. In six months that was up to 500,000. Two years later there were 100 million searches a day. Today, daily Google searches number over 4.4 billion.[4]

Google is the king of search and a profit-making machine. It could easily have continued to focus on search for a long, long time. But that is not how a visionary like Page operates.

Instead, he rethought the future and decided to make changes to capitalize on the impending waves of opportunity beyond search. In August of 2015, Page released a letter announcing a reorganization of Google into multiple companies under a parent entity called Alphabet. Why mess with a good thing? Why risk rethinking a company that is clearly one of the most successful in the world?

As Page said when the company went public in 2004, "Google is not a conventional company. We do not intend to become one."[5] Page expanded on that philosophy when answering those questions in his letter announcing the change.

"We've long believed that over time companies tend to get comfortable doing the same thing, just making incremental changes," he wrote. "But in the technology industry, where revolutionary ideas drive the next big growth areas, you need to be a bit uncomfortable to stay relevant."[6]

Page's idea is that individual companies can innovate faster than a single large enterprise. The original Google still focuses on search and together with the related divisions Ads, YouTube, Apps, Android, and Maps make up one of 12 companies under the Alphabet umbrella today. The others branch out into new areas, including:

- Smart home devices and the Internet of Things (Nest)
- Energy, internet access, fiber (Access and Energy)
- Healthcare and disease prevention (Verily)
- Longevity and life expansion (Calico)
- Urban innovation (Sidewalk Labs)
- Technology incubator tackling geopolitical challenges (Jigsaw)
- Venture capital (GV)
- Growth equity for portfolio companies (Google Capital)
- Artificial intelligence (Google Deep Mind)
- Self-driving cars (Google Self Driving Car Project)

And, of course, there had to be a company for Page's beloved moonshots – X. Some of these new divisions and some of X's moonshots have hit potholes on the road to the future, and that is to be expected from such an array of ambitious endeavors. Early results for Alphabet overall, however, have been strong. Page is betting that the commitment to innovation will pay off down the road in a major way. For now, Alphabet earned close to $19.5 billion on $90.3 billion in revenue in 2016,[7] a testament to the value of constant transformation and innovation.

While still dominating its core service area of search, Page and Google (er...Alphabet) refuse to stand still, positioning the business for massive future growth.

Sharing The Wealth

Sometimes the future is not just about the money.

Yes, you need revenue and profit to sustain your business, but a number of entrepreneurs have added a social component to their companies and have reaped both financial and societal rewards. They rethought beyond the future of their businesses to the future of the world in which we live.

Blake Mycoskie, founder of TOMS Shoes, is one such visionary. Mycoskie built TOMS on an innovative model to help relieve poverty. TOMS implemented a "one-for-one" business model – for every pair of shoes it sold, it would give away a free pair to someone in need. To date the company has donated more than 70 million pairs of shoes. It more recently moved into sunglasses, and has delivered eye care to hundreds of thousands.

The model has also translated into tremendous business success. For the 2016 fiscal year, Fortune estimated TOMS' revenue at approximately $500 million.[8] This success has not gone unnoticed in the business community. In 2014, Bain paid $300 million for a 50 percent share of the company.

Looking at the one-for-one model, over time Mycoskie realized the business needed to evolve from just giving away shoes to having a real, substantive impact on the ground in local communities. At TOMS' facilities in Kenya, India, and Ethiopia, around 500 locals now produce 40 percent of the company's donated shoes.

In addition, looking at the one-for-one platform he had created, Mycoskie is now attempting to create a one-for-one universe covering many products and markets. After the acquisition, Bain and TOMS took one percent of the company's value – a total of $12.5 million, to start TOMS Social Entrepreneurship Fund to fuel the next generation of social businesses. Mycoskie and his wife added $150 million to the fund.

The dozen companies that have sprung from the fund have been focused on a diverse number of social causes, including helping homeless and disabled artists and making affordable organic food.

Mycoskie told Inc. Magazine he sees his efforts "as part of an expanding ecosystem." He feels the young people who buy TOMS' products "will generate a feeder system. They become customers; and then a certain percentage of them will go work for a social enterprise or start one...That's how a movement is created."[9]

Teaching An Elephant To Dance

Whereas TOMS Shoes was a startup, rethinking change is something that can be done by companies of any age and size, even one already with billions in annual revenue and a massive legacy infrastructure.

For years, IBM was perceived as the gold standard in U.S. business. A familiar saying in purchasing circles was "no one ever got fired for buying IBM."

But the shine began to come off IBM in the mid 1990's. Its mainframe business was being eaten alive by minicomputers and the company had declined precipitously from its peak in the late 1980's. The PC division was also in rough shape, having lost significant market share over the same time period. In 1993, the company posted an $8 billion loss and shares that had sold for $43 in 1987 were down to $12.

Larry Ellison of Oracle said at the time, "IBM? We don't even think about those guys anymore. They're not dead. They're irrelevant."[10]

IBM's problems stemmed from an internally focused culture more concerned with protecting internal fiefdoms than servicing customers.

Enter Lou Gerstner.

The situation was so desperate that the IBM board broke with tradition and for the first time ever hired an outsider as CEO – Gerstner, a former CEO of RJR Nabisco and senior executive at American Express and McKinsey & Co. He came into IBM with the mindset of a former customer, not a technical insider. And that made all the difference. He was not concerned with IBM's past or present; he was focused on rethinking IBM's future.

One of Gerstner's first acts was to scrap a turnaround plan to break IBM into smaller businesses. As a former customer, that made no sense to him. He understood that businesses did not want to have all their eggs in one vendor basket, but they also did not want to have to piece together intricate systems from a myriad of suppliers. Someone had to combine all the components into a working system.

"At the end of the day, in every industry, there's an integrator," Gerstner wrote in his 2002 book *Who Says Elephants Can't Dance.*

He felt the size and reach of IBM made it the perfect company to take on that role.

To do that, he had to dump IBM's proprietary attitude. He recalls in his book that when he was at American Express, IBM withdrew support for a large credit card data center because the manager had installed a single Amdahl computer in a facility that had been operating with 100 percent IBM hardware.

Gerstner understood that IBM no longer ruled the computer hardware roost and to take the company into the future meant leveraging all of Big Blue's assets – hardware and software. The company would now focus on consulting and services, not merely products. Sometimes those solutions required using competitor products, so he committed IBM to open standards.

Thanks to a relentless focus on customer relationships and ruthless cost cutting, IBM was able to show a $382 million profit by the end of 1993. In 1994, the company earned $3 billion on revenue of $64 billion.[11] By 1999, revenue had grown to $87.5 billion with profits of $7.7 billion.[12] IBM's Global Services unit, once an afterthought, grew into a $30 billion business with more than 135,000 employees.[13]

Gerstner left a rejuvenated IBM in 2002, but the rethinking of the company continued. In 2008, as the world was struggling in an economic downturn, IBM initiated its Smarter Planet campaign, further transforming the company from one that sold services, to one that solved the biggest challenges of society, government, and business.

IBM chairman Sam Palmisano announced the Smarter Planet vision of instrumentation, interconnectedness, and intelligence. The goal was "for industries, infrastructure, processes, cities, and entire societies to be more productive, efficient, and responsive."[14]

Some of the projects the initiative dealt with included trying to solve the traffic gridlock in London and improving clinical results and operational efficiency in hospitals and primary care clinics in Spain. It was no longer about the cost of hardware or integrating with the internet. Instead, it was tackling Olympic-sized global challenges and problems.

In 2010, Smarter Planet generated $3 billion in revenue and double-digit growth from more than 6,000 client engagements.[15]

In 2015, Chairman and CEO Ginni Rometty took IBM beyond Smarter Planet with its Cognitive Business campaign, looking towards artificial intelligence (AI) and machine learning as the next big thing to help companies solve the most challenging and complex problems. Forget digital. Think cognitive. "Outthink Risk." "Outthink Competitors." "Outthink Cancer."

Cognitive Business addresses the rapid advances in technology and combines digital business with digital intelligence. "Digital is the wires, but digital intelligence, or artificial intelligence as some people call it, is about much more than that," Rometty said in an interview in *Fortune*. "The next decade is about how you combine those and become a cognitive business."[16]

Constant evolution...

Heading Into The Cloud

More proof that size does not prevent a company from transformation is Amazon. How did a company that started out by selling books end up being a technology and retail giant with close to $136 billion in annual revenue and with a cloud services platform that alone delivers $12.2 billion in its own right?[17] Simple, by rethinking its future during every step of its evolution.

Jeff Bezos' original plan for Amazon when he incorporated the business in 1994 (originally called Cadabra) was to make a wider selection of a product people wanted – books – available in a more convenient shopping channel. He knew physical book stores were limited in what they could carry and that books would be easy to pack and ship without risk of damage. He even located his business close to a major book distributor so he would not have to store inventory.

In 1995 Amazon sold its first book online. A year later Bezos expanded Amazon's reach with an affiliate program followed in 1997 by opening the company's first remote distribution center and offering one-click ordering to simplify the checkout process and lower cart abandonment.

Once he got rolling, Bezos realized Amazon's growing sales and distribution model could be expanded beyond books. In 1998, he moved into music, DVD/video sales and acquired Internet Movie Database, the first step into the power of leveraging information to enhance customer satisfaction.

The year 1998 brought the beginning of sales of home improvement products, software, video games, and gift items. Third-party ordering started in 2000, along with the introduction of toys and photo equipment. That was also the year Amazon began offering free shipping on orders greater than $100.

By 2002, Amazon was humming along, expanding its online retail business, building warehouses, and developing a sophisticated technology infrastructure. Bezos could have been content to continue growing the online retail business but he began to understand the powerful IT environment Amazon had created.

He rethought what he had and expanded in a new direction, leveraging the infrastructure to get into cloud computing. As a result, Amazon Web Services (AWS) was born.

Amazon continued to add more product lines to its retail business and transformed again with the launch of the Kindle e-reader in 2007. The Kindle Fire was released later, launching Amazon into the tablet market.

Amazon is not stopping now. Its latest innovation brings it into the world of the Internet of Things (IoT) with Amazon Echo, better known as Alexa. The blue tooth device turns lights and lawn sprinklers on and off, makes phone calls, gives weather forecasts, reads Kindle books, and plays music.

One of the keys to Amazon's innovative culture is that it is not afraid to try something new. From books to CDs, electronics, and fashion, and from AWS to Kindle e-readers, Amazon Lending, and Alexa, Amazon is continually reinventing itself.

"What's dangerous is not to evolve," stated Bezos. These are wise words, indeed, from a mind that is always rethinking the future of the business.

Growing From Vegetables To The Internet

As mentioned earlier in this chapter, another example showing that it is never too late to rethink your business is Wipro. Most people recognize Wipro as one of India's IT powerhouses with revenues of $7.7 billion in 2016 and a workforce of more than

170,000.[18] As mentioned, though, few realize that Wipro is an acronym for Western India Palm Refined Oils Ltd. The company was founded in 1945 as a manufacturer of vegetable and refined oils in Mumbai, Maharashtra, India. The company's logo still features a sunflower as a throwback to its roots.

So how did it go from vegetable oil to IT services, consulting, and systems integration in the aerospace and automotive industries? By constantly looking to the future and reinventing the company.

Azim Premji, son of the founder who took over the company in 1966, had the foresight to recognize that the world was at the dawn of the computer age and India could be in on the ground floor. In the 70's and 80's, Premji refocused the company on IT and computing opportunities and changed the name to Wipro in 1977.

It continued operating in the consumer products market and launched several new soaps. But Premji kept a keen eye on his growing IT business. In the 1990's, Wipro partnered with global telecom provider Royal Dutch Telecom (KPN) to provide Internet service to India.

In 2000, Wipro formed a massive outsourcing joint venture with KPMG Consulting, and the 2000's then became a period of growth for Wipro. In fact, the company was the fastest wealth creator in India from 1997 to 2002 with its market cap growing 133 percent during the period.[19]

Again looking to the future, Wipro anticipated the shift to green energy and entered the clean energy business with Wipro Eco Energy in 2008.

Now, under new CEO Abidali Neemuchwala, Wipro is again

looking to the future. He is driving a major cultural change in the company in an attempt to regain market leadership. The company is focusing on becoming more consultative to meet the market demand for integrated services. Whereas in the past service lines would focus on the products it was creating, they now focus on intellectual property creation that can be applied more broadly in solving customer challenges.

Noticing that enterprise customers are now expecting the same type of experience with their solutions that Apple has brought to interfaces and Amazon has brought to customer service, Wipro is pushing to become a leader in interface design, artificial intelligence, among other areas.

Wipro has come a long way from vegetable oil and soaps – a direct result of rethinking its future.

Dedicated Time for The Future

As you can see, rethinking the future of your business can take many forms, and it is something that every type of business can, and should, do.

A key aspect of marketing is to understand the market, and that includes the waves of change in the market. The greater your ability to anticipate the future, the greater your ability to capitalize on new opportunities for growth. It is not enough to just take the widget of today and say, "OK, now how should I sell this?" Rather, a true marketing leader rethinks what the company should be selling to meet the needs of the audience. A true marketing leader is a visionary. A true marketing leader is a prognosticator.

But when should you start rethinking the future of your buisness? How do you start? How do you put structure to the process?

It is important that you set aside dedicated time to think of the longer-term, the business that your business will become in the future. At a minimum, this should be evaluated, reviewed, and reconsidered every quarter. Business moves too fast these days to look at the long term only once a year.

As for when to start, what are you doing this afternoon? I am not kidding. Building your two businesses – the one you are working on today and the one you are building for tomorrow – is something that you should always be doing. There is no magic point in time, or a specific point in a company's evolution to start. There is no time to waste in getting started on the future of your business.

As can be seen in many of the examples provided in this book, whether Moz or Basecamp, whether TOMS or Amazon, whether IBM or Wipro, all are masters at transformation. Each is a different business today than when it started.

Opportunities for innovation arise frequently. To put yourself in position to capitalize you should be carving out time to continuously learn about your target audience's frustrations, monitor changes in the industry, learn from other industries, and actively work on your business of tomorrow. Reimagining your future business should be a structured process, not something left to whim or random chance.

At our agency, Stratabeat, this takes the form of offsite quarterly planning meetings where we look at not only the prior quarter's performance and the coming quarter's plans and priorities, we also explore how the agency needs to be evolving longer term.

All of this exploration leads to new services that bring more value to clients, making us a more critical resource for them. For example, when we started, we provided branding, web design, and digital marketing services. What we found was that brand strategy was a gaping hole in the market, with almost every middle market prospect we met in need of it and with very few agencies able to do it effectively. So, we formalized a brand strategy practice, and it is now a sizable percentage of our business. It also acts as a stronger, more strategic foundation for all of our other services, enabling us to generate greater client success.

Brand strategy was not something that was a part of the company during day one, but is now a core strength and a key part of our identity. Without a methodical process of exploring the future needs of our clients, it may never have come to be such an important part of the business.

First, Understand Your Audience Better Than Anyone Else

Now it is your turn to rethink your future. Define a process and dedicate the time to work on your future business.

To identify waves of momentum that your business can ride into the future, start by understanding your audience better than anyone else in your industry.

In the past, you had to rely primarily on focus groups to find out what your customers are doing and thinking. That is no longer the case. Today there are a host of available tools to help you, including:

- Online surveys
- Search data that reveals how people think

- Available market research
- Scalable, outsourced market research solutions
- Social media monitoring
- Content monitoring
- Emotion recognition technology
- Analytics of every kind – for your website, email campaigns, search marketing, content marketing, videos, and advertising campaigns
- Website optimization tools that reveal onsite behavior
- A/B testing – of your website, landing pages, ads, email, etc.
- Most importantly, talk with your customers and other audience members

With the plethora of tools, services, and information available, there is no excuse to not understand your audience in great detail these days. Both quantitative and qualitative information should be combined to provide your brand with the greatest insights.

With all the digital horsepower at your fingertips, though, remember to just talk with folks, as well. Take someone out to lunch or dinner and ask lots of questions. And become an expert at listening, really listening to the frustrations they are trying to eliminate and to the more nuanced goals they are trying to achieve. What do they want their business or their life to look like in the future? Understanding future opportunities is not just about knowledge, it is about being part researcher, part prognosticator, and part psychologist.

Understand Technological Change

In addition to understanding your audience at a deeper level, remember to make use of new marketing technologies. If you ignore the value of marketing technology and choose to do things the old way, you will fall behind, be at a significant disadvantage, and start losing to competitors who leverage new tools.

The Internet changed everything, of course. Microsoft was slow to admit that the Internet was a game changer. They stopped seeing the future and instead clung to the past. Companies like Amazon, Apple, Facebook, and Google capitalized on the opportunity to rethink the new world around us even though at the time it was actually Microsoft that was in the best financial position to forge into any one of these areas.

In marketing, we now have endless tools and technologies underlying everything from data visualization, data management platforms, and attribution, to SEO, content marketing, and PR, to behavioral analysis, landing pages, and conversion optimization. Scott Brinker, co-founder and CTO of ion interactive and author of *Hacking Marketing: Agile Practices to Make Marketing Smarter, Faster, and More Innovative*, covers the changes in marketing technology in his Chief Marketing Technologist Blog. In the blog, Brinker has published a number of marketing technology landscape reports and highly shared graphics. In his 2017 report, Brinker identified 5,381 marketing technology solutions on the market. This compares to roughly 150 in his 2011 report and approximately 350 in his 2012 report.[20] To ignore the trends in this technology explosion would be risky at best.

And if you thought that technology options could not possibly expand beyond this point, fasten your seatbelt. The wave of technology investment in the marketing world is only at the starting line. Ashu Garg, a general partner at the venture capital firm Foundation Capital, in his report *MarTech and the Decade of the CMO*, predicted in February 2015 that marketing technology spend by CMOs will increase 10X in the following 10 years. He wrote, "The data nerd of today is the CMO of tomorrow."[21]

If there was ever a time to focus on technology and its ramifications to your future marketing, now would be it.

Understand the Waves of Change

Technology is only one aspect of the future that is rushing at us at an ever-faster pace. Other waves of change heading our way include:

- **Consumer Expectations** – Consumers want immediate gratification. They want what they want and they want it now, they want it customized, and they want superior service along with it.
- **Customer Experience** – The market is flooded with "me too" products. Delivering a unique, exceptional experience is now becoming a key, competitive advantage.
- **Customer Service** – With barriers to entry falling in most industries, a surefire way to lose customers is to have shoddy customer service. Customer service, though, can be expensive. Some innovative companies are now making do-it-yourself (DIY) support easier, and others are introducing predictive support and proactively reaching out to help when the need is likely to arise.
- **Speed** – Ever accelerating speed is now an expectation of your target market. If your service took three months

in the past, they now expect it in two. Automation, process innovation, and artificial intelligence, among other factors are enabling faster and faster delivery times.

- **Channels** – Sometimes, innovation takes the form of delivering the same products or services in a new, novel way. Think of Amazon selling books online, or LegalZoom offering pre-packaged legal services at the click of a button.
- **Social Business** – Today's buyer wants to know not only what your brand offers, but what you stand for, how you produce your offerings, how you treat your employees, as well as your impact on society.
- **Environmentally-friendly Business** – We have only one chance at sustaining our planet, and this means that businesses will be finding ever-more innovative ways to build environmentally-friendly models.
- **Cross-pollination of Industries** – The integration of ideas or products from two or more industries can be a powerful innovative force in the creation of completely new offerings.
- Etc.

What waves of innovation have you identified? What are you doing to prepare your company to capitalize on them to forge a future competitive edge?

The Next Three Years

Anticipating, changing, and adapting to new conditions and environments is crucial for any business. Change will be affecting marketing organizations, as well. To that end, I had the pleasure of collecting prognostications from a number of marketing leaders to help you see the future of marketing itself.

Introduced to you earlier, Jerome Hiquet, CMO of ToughMudder, sees connecting with customers in different ways as a key challenge, and opportunity, for marketers over the next few years. "With the explosion of social media and digital platforms, it is about finding and creating new ways to reach existing and new customers," Hiquet says. "Video content is increasingly becoming the dominant form by which brands communicate – not to customers, but communities, followers and subscribers. Multi-platform marketing campaigns are essential. It's about creating content people want to watch, engage with and share on their networks.

"Consumers are spending more time on mobile than any other screen and brands need to create content that's easily consumed and socially shareable," Hiquet goes on. "Brands need to be even more creative about the content they're pushing out. Content needs to be sticky and relevant. Consumers need to want to engage with it, share it with their network, and ultimately, want to purchase the product or service.

Viji Davis, CMO at Resolution Media, a digital marketing agency catering to Fortune 500 brands, like Hiquet, sees mobile as a key area upon which to focus in the coming three years. "Mobile is here to stay – every year has been 'the year of mobile' for the past decade," says Davis. "It is now finally and truly the year of mobile, with mobile overtaking the desktop on many fronts. Mobile web usage has already surpassed desktop, with more mobile users than desktop users worldwide. According to Google, there are now more mobile searches than desktop. Mobile will not only become a critical area for marketers in the years to come, it already is."

In addition to mobile, Davis sees hyper customer-centricity as a wave of the future. "Platforms are going to continue to hyper service consumer behavior," Davis continues. Hyper customer-centricity will bring the individual into sharper focus for brands. Marketers will do this through more powerful and sophisticated technologies to track and anticipate customer behavior. This level of granularity will increase in importance over time, as the speed of change and consumer expectations accelerates.

Continuing the theme of customer-centricity, Jeffrey Hayzlett, former CMO of Kodak, Chairman of C-Suite Holdings, and best-selling author, sees a growing sophistication in customer engagement in the coming years. "I see us getting more refined around managing our communities and customer bases," Hayzlett explains. "Engagement around your customer has always been predominately what you should spend most of your time on. However, for a long time we were cheating our customers by being able to shout at them through broadcast, radio, direct mail or email. Today, with the cocooning of our audiences, they can filter out the shouting. You then have to find a way to get more intimate and engaged, so I think you will see a lot more intimacy and engagement by brands in order to reach their target customer."

Ken Yamada, Global Digital Marketing Director at Nike, sees a digitally on-demand future. "In 3 years, consumption of goods, services and media will be on-demand and disassociated with time and location. There is hardly going to be an opportunity to 'interrupt' the consumer with a brand message. Despite this, publishers and platforms are going to continually build avenues for advertising that drive qualified customers for advertisers with one caveat – everything will be digital.

"As a result," Yamada continues, "I believe that marketing will become 100 percent digitally oriented to the extent that any business or brand that lacks the understanding and know-how of inspiring their customers in the digital world to be out of business. Those brands who have built expertise and an understanding of marketing in the digital world will exponentially increase their capabilities through increased automation and real-time data-driven and machine-based decision making. Ad space will be auctioned by the millisecond and any brand incapable of building a strategy to win the share of impression will never be able to cut through the competition."

Other marketing leaders speak to a world growing ever more connected. "We see a future where everything is connected and searchable, in the home, the car, wearables, and more," says Beth LeTendre, CEO at Catalyst, a digital marketing agency serving many Fortune 1000 brands. "Low cost sensors and advances in wireless technology are bringing the world around us online. With a veritable supercomputer in their pocket in the form of a smartphone, consumers now expect connectivity everywhere. And they are going to get it.

"This interconnectedness will transform industry after industry. In healthcare, we'll see greater monitoring and diagnosis capabilities. In automotive, we'll see self-driving cars, intelligent logistics, and greater safety features. In retail, we'll see increased supply chain efficiencies and a more responsive customer experience. Companies that are looking to gain an edge in the future will start planning for the connected world now."

"As our devices get smarter and more connected, so will our capabilities in targeting consumers with customized messaging," states Kerry Curran, Managing Partner of Marketing Integration at Catalyst. "The future of marketing is a more programmatic ad serving capability for both search and display marketing, and smarter analytics that provide more granular insights for more relevant connections with prospective customers."

Looking to the future, Mary Ellen Duggan, CMO of WP Engine, talks of the importance of communicating with your customers in the growing area of content marketing. "Branded content is expected to rise from $10B in 2014 to $25B by 2019," Dugan says. "Creating a strategy to showcase your unique perspective, as well as, implementing a distribution plan across social, mobile, and influencers will be vital to break-through.

"Brands need to stay in front of their customers, but doing so is getting increasingly difficult," Duggan asserts. "Content must provide a clear benefit and must fit the environment in which it appears in a way that feels authentic to consumers."

From my own perspective looking at the coming three years, I believe that artificial intelligence (AI) and emotion detection/recognition will grow in importance across many industries. AI has attracted roughly $17 billion in investment in a recent five-year period, according to the AI analytics firm Quid. Companies that have purchased AI firms include Apple, Yahoo, Intel, Dropbox, LinkedIn, Pinterest, Twitter, and Google. In fact, Google's CEO Sundar Pichai has stated that Google will incorporate AI into every new product it introduces in the future.

Similarly, the emotion detection and recognition market is on a growth path. The market is estimated to surpass $36 billion by the year 2021, according to the market research firm MarketsandMarkets.[22] This is an area that I believe will revolutionize marketing in the years to come.

Apple has been keenly interested in emotion recognition for years now. A few years ago, the company filed a patent that described software for analyzing and identifying a person's mood based on a variety of signals, including facial expression.

More recently, Apple acquired Emotient, an emotion-recognition technology company. Emotient has a patent for a method of collecting and labeling up to 100,000 facial images a day, supporting a computer's ability to recognize facial expressions. It is reasonable to believe that Emotient's emotion recognition technology will start appearing in iPhones and iPads before you know it, and then possibly used as a platform for more targeted and dynamic engagement when users are in their browsers.

Affectiva, an emotion recognition technology developer, has raised $34 million in funding to date. Affectiva boasts the world's largest emotion data repository, with more than 5 million faces analyzed using its technology.

Imagine being able to dynamically change your ad, website, or displays in a trade show booth based on the emotional reaction of your audience. This is made possible with emotion detection and recognition technology such as Affectiva's, and is going to be the norm sooner than you realize. Companies such as Unilever already test thousands of ads using emotion recognition technology to optimize their advertising. CBS uses the technology to analyze promos, ads, and primetime TV show content.

"Initially, the technology was used to understand how consumers engage with their brand content and advertising, and how these emotions then influence brand awareness and purchase intent," says Gabi Zijderveld, CMO at Affectiva. "Now the technology is also used to infuse consumer experiences, apps and interactive advertising with Emotion AI. This will help to transform the face of marketing and advertising by reading human emotions and then adapting consumer experiences to these emotions in real time. The technology gives marketers the power to truly delight and engage their customers with uniquely dynamic and personalized interactions."

In addition to AI and emotion recognition, I see predictive analytics growing in importance in the coming years. Much of the analytics in use today is highly useful, but there is a disconnect between the analytics, based on the past, and the current marketing activities being conducted. Predictive analytics uses techniques such as data mining, modeling, and even AI to make predictions about the future, and it opens new opportunities for automated optimization of marketing initiatives for greater results. With continually growing volumes of data and ever faster and cheaper computing power, predictive analytics will gain momentum in the years ahead, and the brands that learn to master predictive analytics will have a clear competitive advantage.

Beyond all of this, though, I believe that creativity will carry immeasurable value in the world of marketing in the coming years. When you consider the thousands upon thousands of marketing messages that individuals are faced with daily, creativity offers an effective way to cut through all the noise and connect and engage deeply with your audience. Remember the stories of the pasta company and shampoo brand in the chapter *Rethink Your Metrics*. Think of how people gush about Warby Parker. Consider how fiercely loyal Apple customers are. You can use all the technology in the world, but if your message is off or lost in a sea of sameness, your brand's potential will be severely limited.

It is not only your industry that is changing. Marketing itself is changing all around us. It is not whether it will continue to change in the future, but rather how you will adapt, evolve, and innovate to stay ahead of your competition in connecting with and fulfilling the needs of customers. Take the time to define the specific changes you think you will be seeing in the coming three years in your industry. What do you need to do now in order to thrive as the changes gain traction in the market? What are the structures, personnel, and strategies you will need to be successful? In an ideal scenario, what will your business look like in three years?

Now, go make that happen!

Chapter Summary

Change is constant and you need to be thinking about "riding the wave" or you could be washed away by it. You need to envision where the world – and your customers – are going. As strong as your brand may be today, you should continually look to the future to stay ahead of your competition, fulfill customer needs, and ensure your future success. Take the time to understand where your industry, and where marketing itself, will be in the next few years.

Remember, beyond the business that you are building today, you need to be building the business of tomorrow at the same time. Rethink your future, so that it will be full of continued growth and profitability.

- What changes are right around the corner in your industry? What waves of change can you ride for better leverage?
- What new products, services, and solutions would appeal to your customers?
- How can you thrill your customers in the future in ways that even they have never thought of?

- How can you leverage your expertise to enter completely new markets?
- Do you have a structured process for planning the long-term direction of your business?
- How do you see technology in your industry changing in the coming years, and how will you capitalize on such changes?
- Do you recognize the coming changes to the marketing world itself, and how will you evolve your own marketing to capitalize on the changes?
- What should your business look like in three years for you to have a powerful competitive edge?

CONCLUSION

I hope that you enjoyed the strategies and stories outlined throughout *Rethink Your Marketing*. My goal with the book was to highlight effective methods to jumpstart growth for your business, and I hope that you have gained new ideas to engage more deeply with your audience, outsmart the competition, and ignite new revenue growth.

As mentioned in the book, when the market changed, Domino's reinvented itself and launched a 360° marketing campaign to include everyone in the process. Since the Pizza Turnaround, Domino's has been the fastest-growing restaurant in the United States. Not just among pizza brands or just among fast food chains, but among *all* restaurants.

Marlin Steel targeted a different audience, and its revenue increased by 10X.

Jon Spoelstra introduced dunking sumo wrestlers at New Jersey Nets basketball games, and cranked up overall revenue for the NBA franchise by almost 500 percent within three years.

WP Engine increased its content marketing by 10X, and then

proceeded to add more than 20,000 new customers in a single year.

Legendary Entertainment rethought its analytics, even hiring a Harvard astrophysicist. It transformed how movies are marketed through applied data analytics, culminating in the $3.5 billion acquisition of the company.

If your business is stuck or you have hit a plateau, rethink your marketing to unleash revenue growth. Merely tweaking what you are doing, though, will most likely lead to stagnation. Merely copying what the competition is doing will result in frustration. Merely following what the media is hyping will lead to failure.

When rethinking your marketing, go big. Think boldly. In the many examples presented in this book, you see that success comes to the courageous.

Be fearless, rethink your marketing, and transform your business.

NOTES

INTRODUCTION

1 Joseph Durso, "Fearless Fosbury Flops to Glory," *The New York Times*, http://ow.ly/KwAz30dPsZX

2 "Dick Fosbury," *Wikipedia*, https://en.wikipedia.org/wiki/Dick_Fosbury

RETHINK YOUR AUDIENCE

1 Alex Turnbull, "How Grasshopper Scrapped Their Way To $30M+ In Annual Revenue," Groove blog, https://www.groovehq.com/blog/grasshopper-david-hauser-interview

2 Scott Kirsner, "Unicorns may get all the attention, but Grasshopper shows the benefits of focusing on customers," *Beta-Boston*, http://www.betaboston.com/news/2015/11/12/unicorns-

may-get-all-the-attention-but-grasshopper-shows-the-benefits-of-growing-slowly/

3 Kristan Schiller, "Can Ignoring Clients Boost Your Sales," *Entrepreneur*, https://www.entrepreneur.com/article/226744

4 "Imprivata Agrees To Be Acquired By Thoma Bravo," Imprivata website, https://www.imprivata.com/company/press/imprivata-agrees-be-acquired-thoma-bravo

5 Eric Siu, "How Mark Organ's Eloqua Nearly Ended Up Bankrupt," *Entrepreneur*, https://www.entrepreneur.com/article/269856

6 "Bill Gross: A Devotion to New Ideas," *Stanford eCorner*, https://www.youtube.com/watch?v=EdTj6JLxryo

7 Sheila Marikar, "How You Make $8.5 Million As a Popcorn Company," *Inc.*, https://www.inc.com/magazine/201604/sheila-marikar/popcorn-palace-timothy-heitmann-strategy.html

8 Charles Fishman, "The Road To Resilience: How Unscientific Innovation Saved Marlin Steel," *Fast Company*, https://www.fastcompany.com/3012591/marlin-steel-metal-baskets

9 John Grossmann, "From Making Bagel Baskets to Thinking Much Bigger," *The New York Times*, https://www.nytimes.com/2014/05/01/business/smallbusiness/from-making-bagel-baskets-to-rethinking-small-manufacturing-in-america.html

10 "Tableau Reports Q4 and Full Year 2016 Financial Results," *PR Newswire*, http://www.prnewswire.com/news-releases/tableau-reports-q4-and-full-year-2016-financial-results-300401534.html

11 Zoe Henry, "ZenPayroll Gets Sexy With Benefits...and a Name Change," *Inc.*, http://www.inc.com/zoe-henry/zenpayroll-launches-health-benefits-tool.html

12 Chris Zook and James Allen, "Growth Outside the Core," *Harvard Business Review*, https://hbr.org/2003/12/growth-outside-the-core

13 Liz Welch, "'Shark Tank' Star Robert Herjavec on Mark Cuban: 'If He Did It, Why Not Me?'," *Inc.*, http://www.inc.com/magazine/201607/liz-welch/robert-herjavec-shark-tank-better-entrepreneur.html

14 Ben Parr, "Facebook Paid $8.5 Million to Acquire Fb.com," *Mashable*, http://mashable.com/2011/01/11/facebook-paid-8-5-million-to-acquire-fb-com/

15 "Facebook Reports Fourth Quarter and Full Year 2016 Results," Facebook website, https://investor.fb.com/investor-news/press-release-details/2017/facebook-Reports-Fourth-Quarter-and-Full-Year-2016-Results/default.aspx

16 "Fitbit Reports $574M Q416 and $2.17B FY16 Revenue, Sells 6.5M devices in Q416 and 22.3M devices in FY16," Fitbit website, https://investor.fitbit.com/press/press-releases/press-release-details/2017/Fitbit-Reports-574M-Q416-and-217B-FY16-Revenue-Sells-65M-devices-in-Q416-and-223M-devices-in-FY16/default.aspx

17 Parmy Olson, "Fitbit's Game Plan For Making Your Company Healthy," *Forbes*, http://www.forbes.com/sites/parmyolson/2016/01/08/fitbit-wearables-corporate-wellness/

18 Stephanie D. Smith, "Essence Panel Explores Beauty Purchasing," *WWD*, http://wwd.com/beauty-industry-news/color-cosmetics/essence-panel-explores-beauty-purchasing-2139829/

19 "L'Oreal Annual Report 2016," L'Oreal website, http://www.loreal-finance.com/en/annual-report-2016/key-figures

20 Heidi MacDonald, "Comics and graphic novel sales top $1 billion in 2015," *The Beat*, http://www.comicsbeat.com/comics-and-graphic-novel-sales-top-1-billion-in-2015/

21 Gus Lubin, "The Comic Book Industry Is On Fire, And It's About More Than Just The Movies," *Business Insider*, http://www.businessinsider.com/the-comic-book-industry-is-on-fire-2014-8

22 "Revenue of Converse worldwide from 2010 to 2016 (in million U.S. dollars)," *Statista*, https://www.statista.com/statistics/241850/sales-of-nikes-non-nike-brands-2006-2010/

RETHINK HOW THEY THINK

1 Jeremy Hsu, "Estimate: Human Brain 30 Times Faster than Best Supercomputers," *IEEE Spectrum*,

http://spectrum.ieee.org/tech-talk/computing/networks/estimate-human-brain-30-times-faster-than-best-supercomputers

2 Susan Weinschenk, *Neuro Web Design: What Makes Them Click*, https://www.amazon.com/Neuro-Web-Design-Makes-Click/dp/0321603605

3 Dorie Clark, "Expert Series: Dorie Clark interviews Dr. Robert Cialdini," *Marketing Strategy with Dorie Clark Podcast*, https://www.podomatic.com/podcasts/dorieclark/episodes/2012-01-02T09_27_49-08_00

4 Hilke Passmann, John O'Doherty, Baba Shiv, and Antonio Rangel, "Marketing actions can modulate neural representations of experienced pleasantness," *Proceedings of the National Academy of Sciences*, http://www.pnas.org/content/105/3/1050.full.pdf

5 Antonio Damasio, *Descartes' Error: Emotion, Reason, and the Human Brain*, https://www.amazon.com/Descartes-Error-Emotion-Reason-Human/dp/014303622X

6 Martin Windstorm, "You Love Your iPhone. Literally.," *The New York Times*, http://www.nytimes.com/2011/10/01/opinion/you-love-your-iphone-literally.html

7 Geraldine E. Willigan, "High-Performance Marketing: An Interview with Nike's Phil Knight," *Harvard Business Review*, https://hbr.org/1992/07/high-performance-marketing-an-interview-with-nikes-phil-knight

8 Simon Sinek, *Start With Why,*
https://startwithwhy.com/shop/books/start-with-why

9 Forrester, "Emotion Is Your Top Loyalty Driver,
https://www.youtube.com/watch?v=JDlZOqoUoew

10 CEB and Google, "From Promotion to Emotion: Connecting
B2B Customers to Brands,"
https://www.cebglobal.com/content/dam/cebglobal/us/EN/best-
practices-decision-support/marketing-
communications/pdfs/promotion-emotion-whitepaper-full.pdf

11 Claire Cain Miller, "Google Bases a Campaign on Emotions,
Not Terms," *The New York Times,*
http://www.nytimes.com/2012/01/02/technology/google-hones-
its-advertising-message-playing-to-emotions.html

12 Hamish Pringle and Peter Field, *Brand Immortality: How
Brands Can Live Long and Prosper*, https://www.amazon.-
com/Brand-Immortality-Brands-Live-Prosper/dp/0749449284/

13 David Brandt, "Emotions Give a Lift to Advertising," Nielsen
website,
http://www.nielsen.com/content/dam/nielsenglobal/eu/docs/pdf/
whats-next-emotions-give-a-lift-to-advertising-jan-2016.pdf

14 Robert B. Zajonc, "ATTITUDINAL EFFECTS OF MERE
EXPOSURE," American Psychological Association's *Journal of
Personality and Social Psychology Monograph Supplement, Volume
9, No. 2, Part 2,*
http://www.morilab.net/gakushuin/Zajonc_1968.pdf

15 Gregory S. Berns, M.D., Ph.D, "Human Brain Loves Surprises,

Research Reveals," *ScienceDaily*,
https://www.sciencedaily.com/releases/2001/04/010415224316.htm

16 Alexandre N. Tuch, Eva E. Presslaber, Markus Stockily, Klaus
Opwis, Javier A. Bargas-Avila, "The role of visual complexity and
prototypicality regarding first impression of websites: Working
towards understanding aesthetic judgments," University of
Basel, Department of Psychology, Center for Cognitive
Psychology and Methodology and Google/YouTube,
https://static.googleusercontent.com/media/research.google.com
/en/us/pubs/archive/38315.pdf

17 "Project Superbrand: 10 Truths Reshaping the Corporate
World," Havas Worldwide website,
http://mag.havasww.com/prosumer-report/superbrand/

18 "Authentic 100," Cohn & Wolfe, http://www.authentic100.com/

19 John Medina, *Brain Rules*, http://www.brainrules.net/

20 "POLISHING YOUR PRESENTATION," 3M,
http://web.archive.org/web/20001102203936/http:/3m.com/meetin
gnetwork/files/meetingguide_pres.pdf

21 John Medina, *Brain Rules*, http://www.brainrules.net/

22 John Medina, *Brain Rules*, http://www.brainrules.net/

23 "The Brady Bunch – Oh My Nose!," CBS,
https://www.youtube.com/watch?v=r9nSSrOp6ck

24 *The Armstrong Lie*, Sony Pictures Classics,
http://sonyclassics.com/thearmstronglie/

25 Amos Tversky and Daniel Kahneman, "LOSS AVERSION IN DISKLESS CHOICE: A REFERENCE-DEPENDENT MODEL," http://www3.uah.es/econ/MicroDoct/Tversky_Kahneman_1991_L oss%20aversion.pdf

26 Stuart Wolpert, "How Does Your Brain Respond When You Think about Gambling or Taking Risks? UCLA Study Offers New Insights," UCLA website, http://newsroom.ucla.edu/releases/How-Does-Your-Brain-Respond-When-7680

RETHINK YOUR GOALS

1 Michael Dorame, "OKRs are Old News — Introducing Goal Science Thinking," https://www.linkedin.com/pulse/okrs-old-news-introducing-goal-science-thinking-michael-dorame

2 "Study Focuses on Strategies for Achieving Goals, Resolutions," Dominican University website, http://www.dominican.edu/dominicannews/study-highlights-strategies-for-achieving-goals

3 Edwin Locke and Gary Latham, "Building a Practically Useful Theory of Goal Setting and Task Motivation," *American Psychologist*, http://www-2.rotman.utoronto.ca/facbios/file/09 - Locke & Latham 2002 AP.pdf

4 Rand Fishkin, "Vision-Based Framework," Moz website, https://moz.com/rand/vision-based-framework/

5 Rand Fishkin, "Lessons Learned Growing Moz,"

http://www.slideshare.net/randfish/growing-moz-8-lessons-learned

6 Sarah Bird, "The Moz 2016 Annual Report," Moz website, https://moz.com/blog/the-moz-2016-annual-report

7 Michael Dorame, "OKRs are Old News — Introducing Goal Science Thinking," https://www.linkedin.com/pulse/okrs-old-news-introducing-goal-science-thinking-michael-dorame

8 Hannah Bae, "Bill Gates' 40th anniversary email: 'goal was a computer on every desk'," *CNN Money*, http://money.cnn.com/2015/04/05/technology/bill-gates-email-microsoft-40-anniversary/index.html

9 Robert Strohmeyer, "The 7 Worst Tech Predictions of All Time," *PCWorld*, http://www.pcworld.com/article/155984/worst_tech_predictions.html

10 *Microsoft Annual Report 2016*, Microsoft website, https://www.microsoft.com/investor/reports/ar16/index.html

11 Charlie Sorrel, "More Ballmer Madness: "There's No Chance That the iPhone Is Going to Get Any Significant Market Share. No Chance.," *Wired*, https://www.wired.com/2007/05/more_ballmer_ma/

12 "comScore Reports December 2013 U.S. Smartphone Subscriber Market Share," *comScore*, http://www.comscore.com/Insights/Press-Releases/2014/2/comScore-Reports-December-2013-US-Smartphone-Subscriber-Market-Share

13 Robert Sher, *Mighty Midsized Companies: How Leaders Overcome 7 Silent Growth Killers*, http://www.ceotoceo.biz/newbook.html

14 Robert Sher, "Tinkering with Strategy Can Derail Midsize Companies," *Harvard Business Review*, https://hbr.org/2014/04/tinkering-with-strategy-can-derail-midsize-companies

15 Darren Hardy, *The Compound Effect*, https://www.darrenhardy.com/tcebook/

16 Betsy Morris, "Steve Jobs speaks out," *Fortune*, http://archive.fortune.com/galleries/2008/fortune/0803/gallery.jobsqna.fortune/6.html

17 "Steve Jobs' Advice to Nike: Get Rid of the Crappy Stuff," *Fast Company*, https://www.youtube.com/watch?v=SOCKp9eij3A

18 Sean Covey, Chris McChesney, Jim Huling, *The 4 Disciplines of Execution: Achieving Your Wildly Important Goals*, https://www.franklincovey.com/books.html

19 Scott, "Warren Buffett's 5-Step Process for Prioritizing True Success (and Why Most People Never Do it)," Live Your Legend website, http://liveyourlegend.net/warren-buffetts-5-step-process-for-prioritizing-true-success-and-why-most-people-never-do-it/

20 Jim Collins, *Good to Great: Why Some Companies Make the Leap... And Others Don't*, https://www.harpercollins.com/9780066620992/good-to-great

21 Charles Duhigg, *Smarter Faster Better: The Transformative Power of Real Productivity*, http://charlesduhigg.com/books/smarter-faster-better/

22 Stephen M. Garcia and Avishalom Tor, "The N-Effect: More Competitors, Less Competition," *Association for Psychological Science*, http://www-personal.umich.edu/~smgarcia/pubs/n-effect.pdf

23 Tamao Matsui, Akinori Okada, and Osamu Inoshita, "Mechanism of feedback affecting task performance," *Organizational Behavior and Human Performance*, http://www.sciencedirect.com/science/article/pii/0030507383901150

24 Dr. Heidi Grant Halvorson, *9 Things Successful People Do Differently*, http://www.heidigrantphd.com/books/nine-things-successful-people-do-differently

RETHINK YOUR MARKETING MIX

1 Jon Spoelstra, *Marketing Outrageously*, http://www.jonspoelstra.com/my-marketing-books.html

2 "Arby's wraps 17 above average-industry quarters," *QSRweb*, https://www.qsrweb.com/news/arbys-wraps-17-above-industry-average-quarters/

3 Kate Vinton, "How Two Dermatologists Built a Billion Dollar Brand in Their Spare Time," *Forbes*,

http://www.forbes.com/sites/katevinton/2016/06/01/billion-dollar-brand-proactiv-rodan-fields/

4 DMN Editorial Team, "Five Minutes With: Content is Still King, says Mary Ellen Dugan," *DMN*, http://www.dmnews.com/marketing-automation/five-minutes-with-content-is-still-king-says-mary-ellen-dugan/article/523262/

5 H Li, "A Legendary Approach to Data Analytics," *Harvard Business School*, https://digit.hbs.org/submission/a-legendary-approach-to-data-analytics/

6 H Li, "A Legendary Approach to Data Analytics," *Harvard Business School*, https://digit.hbs.org/submission/a-legendary-approach-to-data-analytics/

7 Natalie Robehmed, "With $3.5B Deal For Legendary Entertainment, Chinese Billionaire Is Pursuing Trans-Pacific Vertical Integration," *Forbes*, http://www.forbes.com/sites/natalierobehmed/2016/01/12/dalian-wanda-group-acquires-thomas-tulls-legendary-entertainment-for-3-5-billion/

8 Patrick J. Sauer, "Confessions of a Viral Video Superstar," *Inc.*, http://www.inc.com/articles/2008/06/blendtec.html

9 Raffi Khatchadourian, "We Know How You Feel," *The New Yorker*, http://www.newyorker.com/magazine/2015/01/19/know-feel

10 Ivana Kottasova, "How to build a $100 million company out of mud," *CNN*,

http://money.cnn.com/2015/11/12/smallbusiness/tough-mudder-endurance-sport/index.html

11 Keith Loria, "Digital No Obstacle for Tough Mudder CMO," *CMO.com*, http://www.cmo.com/interviews/articles/2016/9/21/the-cmo-interview-jerome-hiquet-cmo-tough-mudder.html

12 Amy Gesenhues, "A CMO's View: The Down And Dirty Details On Tough Mudder's Video Marketing Strategy," *Marketing Land*, http://marketingland.com/cmos-view-dirty-details-tough-mudders-video-marketing-strategy-118318

13 Keith Loria, "Digital No Obstacle for Tough Mudder CMO," *CMO.com*, http://www.cmo.com/interviews/articles/2016/9/21/the-cmo-interview-jerome-hiquet-cmo-tough-mudder.html

14 "Growth Process Toolkit," Frost & Sullivan website, https://ww2.frost.com/files/7414/1391/2726/Strategic_Partnerships.pdf

15 Brian Withers, "Two Charts That Show That Shopify Is Built for Growth," *The Motley Fool*, https://www.fool.com/investing/2016/12/08/two-charts-that-show-shopify-is-built-for-growth.aspx

16 "Jerome's Furniture sees 10x times better conversion after implementing LiveChat," LiveChat website, https://www.livechatinc.com/customers/customer-stories/jeromes-furniture/

RETHINK YOUR METRICS

1 "Chamath Palihapitiya - how we put Facebook on the path to 1 billion users," https://www.youtube.com/watch?v=raIUQP7iSBU

2 Lee Caraher, "Pay Attention to Consumer Behavior, with Dave Karraker," *Focus Is Your Friend: How to double down on marketing that matters podcast*, http://www.stitcher.com/podcast/focus-is-your-friend-how-to-double-down-on-marketing-that-matters/e/episode-24-pay-attention-to-consumer-behavior-with-dave-karraker-48768218

RETHINK YOUR REVENUE MODEL

1 Chris Zook and James Allen, "The Great Repeatable Business Model," *Harvard Business Review*, https://hbr.org/2011/11/the-great-repeatable-business-model

2 Saul Kaplan, "How to not get 'Netflixed,'" *Fortune*, http://fortune.com/2011/10/11/how-not-to-get-netflixed/

3 Mike Snider, "Netflix shares hit record after subscriber surge," *USA Today*, http://www.usatoday.com/story/tech/news/2017/01/18/netflix-shares-up-q4-subscriber-additions/96710172/

4 Adam Hartung, "Netflix – The Turnaround Story of 2012!," *Forbes*, http://www.forbes.com/sites/adamhartung/2013/01/29/netflix-the-turnaround-story-of-2012/

5 Eugene Kim, "CEO of $50 billion Salesforce shared his epic founding story to inspire a small business owner," *Business*

Insider, http://www.businessinsider.com/salesforce-benioff-
shares-founding-story-2015-9

6 Erin Trimble, "Salesforce.com: From SaaS Pioneer to Platform
Play," *Harvard Business School OpenForum*,
https://openforum.hbs.org/challenge/understand-digital-
transformation-of-business/business-model/salesforce-com-
from-saas-pioneer-to-platform-play

7 Investor Relations, Salesforce.com website,
http://investor.salesforce.com/about-us/investor/financials/

8 Randy Picker, "Gillette's Strange History with the Razor and
Blade Strategy," *Harvard Business Review*,
https://hbr.org/2010/09/gillettes-strange-history-with

9 Adam Lashinsky, "How Dollar Shave Club got started,"
Fortune, http://fortune.com/2015/03/10/dollar-shave-club-
founding/

10 Mike Isaac and Michael J. de la Merced, "Dollar Shave Club
Sells to Unilever for $1 Billion," *New York Times*,
https://www.nytimes.com/2016/07/20/business/dealbook/unilever
-dollar-shave-club.html

11 David Pakman, "Dollar Shave Club: How Michael Dubin
Created A Massively Successful Company and Re-Defined
CPG," *Medium*, https://medium.com/@pakman/dollar-shave-
club-how-michael-dubin-created-a-massively-successful-
company-and-re-defined-cpg-f2fa700af62b

12 Unaudited Condensed Consolidated Statements of Operations, Apple, Inc.,

http://images.apple.com/newsroom/pdfs/Q4FY16ConsolidatedFi
nancialStatements.pdf

13 Alyson Shontell, "How Getting Mugged And Maced Helped a
World-Class Dancer Save Her Struggling Startup," *Business
Insider*, http://www.businessinsider.com/how-payal-kadakia-
found-success-with-classpass-2014-7

14 Chloe Sorvino, "Why Failing Twice Helped ClassPass's Payal
Kadakia Build a $50 Million (And Growing) Fortune," *Forbes*,
https://www.forbes.com/sites/chloesorvino/2016/06/17/why-
failing-twice-helped-classpasss-payal-kadakia-build-a-50-
million-and-growing-fortune/#5b609d6e36a9

15 Maya Kosoff, "ClassPass, a startup that gym rats and investors
love, is now a $400 million company," *Business Insider*,
http://www.businessinsider.com/classpass-400-million-
valuation-2015-5

16 Chloe Sorvino, "Why Failing Twice Helped ClassPass's
Payal Kadakia Build a $50 Million (And Growing) Fortune,"
Forbes,
https://www.forbes.com/sites/chloesorvino/2016/06/17/why-
failing-twice-helped-classpasss-payal-kadakia-build-a-50-
million-and-growing-fortune/#5b609d6e36a9

17 Jordan Crook, "Fritz Lanman takes CEO role at ClassPass as
founder Payal Kadakia steps in as Chairman," *TechCrunch*,
https://techcrunch.com/2017/03/17/classpass-ceo-fritz-lanman-
payal-kadakia/

18 R.L. Adams, "How Rand Fishkin Created An SEO Empire:
The Story of Moz.com," *Forbes*,

http://www.forbes.com/sites/robertadams/2016/09/06/how-rand-fishkin-created-an-seo-sempire-the-story-of-moz-com/

19 Sarah Bird, "The Moz 2016 Annual Report," Moz website, https://moz.com/blog/the-moz-2016-annual-report

20 François Lanthier Nadeau, "How a tiny pricing change (not a growth hack) tripled revenues," Baremetrics website, https://baremetrics.com/blog/tiny-pricing-change-tripled-revenues

21 François Lanthier Nadeau, "How a tiny pricing change (not a growth hack) tripled revenues," Baremetrics website, https://baremetrics.com/blog/tiny-pricing-change-tripled-revenues

22 Snipcart website, https://snipcart.com/

23 Gerardo A. Dada, "A Pricing Lesson from the Concorde," *The Adaptive Marketer*, https://theadaptivemarketer.com/2012/01/14/a-pricing-lesson-from-the-concorde/

24 "How I doubled the price of my software product – and sold ten times as many copies," *The Startup Project*, http://www.startupproject.org/2011/06/price/

25 "Expert Series: Dorie Clark interviews Dr. Robert Cialdini," *Marketing Strategy with Dorie Clark Podcast*, https://www.podomatic.com/podcasts/dorieclark/episodes/2012-01-02T09_27_49-08_00

26 Michael V. Marn, Eric V. Roegner, and Craig C. Zawada, "The power of pricing," *McKinsey Quarterly*,

http://www.mckinsey.com/business-functions/marketing-and-sales/our-insights/the-power-of-pricing

27 Gregory B. Northcraft and Margaret A. Neale, "Experts, Amateurs, and Real Estate: An Anchoring-and-Adjustment Perspective on Property Pricing Decisions", University of Arizona, http://web.missouri.edu/segerti/capstone/northcraft_neale.pdf

28 Ryan T. Howell Ph.D., "Commas and Cents: Why $1,999.00 is More Than $1999," *Psychology Today*, https://www.psychologytoday.com/blog/cant-buy-happiness/201208/commas-and-cents-why-199900-is-more-1999

RETHINK YOUR FUTURE

1 Wipro website, http://www.wipro.com/about-wipro/

2 "When Digital Disruption Strikes: How Can Incumbents Respond," Capgemini Consulting, https://www.capgemini-consulting.com/resource-file-access/resource/pdf/digital_disruption_1.pdf

3 Panasonic website, http://www.panasonic.com/global/corporate/history/konosuke-matsushita.html

4 Alexander Clark, "Search Engine Statistics," *Smart Insights*, http://www.smartinsights.com/search-engine-marketing/search-engine-statistics/

5 Harry McCracken, "The Invention of Alphabet is the Ultimate Larry Page Move," *Fast Company*, https://www.fastcompany.com/3049693/the-invention-of-alphabet-is-the-ultimate-larry-page-move

6 "Learning Larry Page's Alphabet," *Fast Company*, https://www.fastcompany.com/3057414/learning-larry-pages-alphabet-with-a-little-help-from-microsoft-nike-ge-facebook-and-google

7 "Alphabet Announces Fourth Quarter and Fiscal Year 2016 Results," Alphabet website, https://abc.xyz/investor/news/earnings/2016/Q4_alphabet_earnings/

8 Jeremy Quittner, "What the Founder of TOMS Shoes Is Doing Now," *Fortune*, http://fortune.com/2016/09/08/what-the-founder-of-toms-shoes-is-doing-now/

9 Leigh Buchanan, "What's Next for Toms, the $400 Million For-Profit Built on Karmic Capital," *Inc.*, http://www.inc.com/magazine/201605/leigh-buchanan/toms-founder-blake-mycoskie-social-entrepreneurship.html

10 "Lou Gerstner's Turnaround Tales at IBM," *Knowledge@Wharton*, http://knowledge.wharton.upenn.edu/article/lou-gerstners-turnaround-tales-at-ibm/

11 "IBM Annual Report 1994," ftp://public.dhe.ibm.com/annual-report/1994/ibm1994.pdf

12 "IBM Announces 1999 Fourth-Quarter, Full-Year Results,"

IBM website, https://www-03.ibm.com/press/us/en/pressrelease/1909.wss

13 Gary Hamel, "Waking Up IBM: How a Gang of Unlikely Rebels Transformed Big Blue," Harvard Business Review, https://hbr.org/2000/07/waking-up-ibm-how-a-gang-of-unlikely-rebels-transformed-big-blue

14 "IBM's 100 Icons of Progress," IBM website, http://www-03.ibm.com/ibm/history/ibm100/us/en/icons/smarterplanet/

15 "Smarter Planet," IBM website, http://www-03.ibm.com/ibm/history/ibm100/us/en/icons/smarterplanet/

16 Laura Lorenzetti, "Ginni Rometty: Forget digital – cognitive business is the future," *Fortune*, http://fortune.com/2015/10/13/ginni-rometty-cognitive-business/

17 Taylor Soper, "Amazon Web Services posts $3.5B in sales, up 47% from last year, reaches $14B annual run rate," *GeekWire*, http://www.geekwire.com/2017/amazon-web-services-posts-3-5b-revenue-47-last-year/

18 "About Wipro > Company Overview," Wipro website, http://www.wipro.com/about-Wipro/

19 "Wipro is Fastest Wealth Creator for 5 Years: Study," *The Financial Express*, http://www.financialexpress.com/archive/wipro-is-fastest-wealth-creator-for-5-years-study/68646/

20 Scott Brinker, "Marketing Technology Landscape Super-graphic (2017): Martech 5000" *Chief Marketing Technologist Blog*,

http://chiefmartec.com/2017/05/marketing-techniology-landscape-supergraphic-2017/

21 Ashu Garg, "MarTech and the Decade of the CMO," Foundation Capital website, https://foundationcapital.com/wp-content/uploads/2016/07/DotCMO_whitepaper.pdf

22 "Emotion Detection and Recognition Market by Technology (Bio-Sensor, NLP, Machine Learning), Software Tool (Facial Expression, Voice Recognition), Service, Application Area, End User, and Region - Global Forecast to 2021," MarketsandMarkets website, http://www.marketsandmarkets.com/Market-Reports/emotion-detection-recognition-market-23376176.html

ABOUT THE AUTHOR

Tom Shapiro is Founder and CEO of Stratabeat, Inc. (https://stratabeat.com/), a branding, design, and marketing agency in the greater Boston area. Through his career, Shapiro has developed marketing strategies for more than a dozen Fortune 500 clients, such as Hewlett-Packard, AT&T, Intel, Kraft Foods, eBay, Ameriprise, UnitedHealthcare, and P&G.

Previously, Shapiro was the Director of Digital Strategy at the digital marketing agency iProspect. During his five years at the firm, the number of employees grew from 85 to more than 700. Prior to that, Shapiro was responsible for the U.S. go-to-market strategy for a British software localization firm, tripling overall revenue for the company.

Shapiro's marketing insights have been published in CMO.com, CNN.com, Forbes, HubSpot Blog, iMedia Connection, Internet Retailer, MarketingProfs, MediaPost, National Center for the Middle Market, REALTOR Magazine, Website Magazine, among others.

Follow Shapiro on Twitter at @TomShapiro and @Stratabeat.

ADDITIONAL RESOURCES

Rethink Your Marketing provides you with seven strategies to get unstuck, jumpstart your business, and drive accelerated revenue growth. For additional insights, tools, strategies, and bonus materials, sign up for the *Rethink Your Marketing* mailing list here:

https://rethinkyourmarketing.com/